THE MOUNTAIN AND THE FATHERS
GROWING UP ON THE BIG DRY

THE MOUNTAIN AND THE FATHERS

GROWING UP ON THE BIG DRY

A MEMOIR

JOE WILKINS

COUNTERPOINT | BERKELEY

Portions of this manuscript previously appeared in *American Cowboy*, *Brevity*, *The Briar Cliff Review*, *Ecotone*, *The Georgia Review*, *High Desert Journal*, *Orion*, *The Southern Review*, *The Sun*, and *Terrain*.

With privacy in mind, certan names and identifying details have been changed, and some characters have been rendered as composites.

The Library of Congress has cataloged the hardcover edition as follows:
Wilkins, Joe.
The mountain and the fathers : growing up on the Big Dry / Joe Wilkins.
    p. cm.
ISBN 978-1-58243-794-1
1. Bull Mountain Region (Mont.)—Social conditions. 2. Bull Mountain Region (Mont.)—
    Biography. 3. Rural poor—Montana—Bull Mountain Region. 4. Droughts—Social aspects—
    Montana—Bull Mountain Region. 5. Wilkins, Joe—Childhood and youth. I. Title.
F737.B85W55 2012
978.6'39—dc23   2011039682

Paperback ISBN: 978-1-61902-161-7

Cover design by Michael Kellner
Book Interior by Maria E. Torres, Neuwirth & Associates, Inc.
Printed in the United States of America

COUNTERPOINT
2560 Ninth Street, Suite 318
Berkeley, CA 94710
www.counterpointpress.com
Distributed by Publishers Group West

10 9 8 7 6 5 4 3

For my children—
Walter James Wilkins
and *Edith Marilyn Wilkins*—

what names you carry.

PROLOGUE

NIGHT

WHAT I REMEMBER without qualification is the dark.

What I remember is being pulled from the dark of sleep by my grandfather—I can just see the wide, shadowing brim of his gray felt hat—and placed gently in the sheepskin-lined backseat of my grandparents' Oldsmobile. What I remember is my little brother, his small, warm body next to me, and beside him my straight-backed, unsmiling older sister. She is thirteen and understands what this is all about and so has buried her face in her hands. What I remember is being pulled from the dark of sleep and into the dark of deep winter midnight in eastern Montana.

What I remember are the Oldsmobile's headlights carving out the dark, hollowing the space before us: two-lane highway, arms of winter cottonwood, quick flash of a sand-rock ridge and the Bull Mountains beyond. Does my grandfather tap the brake as we slip around the ess curves above the river? What yellow eyes are those near the culvert? Jackrabbit? Skunk? Maybe coyote? Is my brother crying now, too? I don't know, I don't know—I can see some way into the dark, but no farther.

What I remember is a dry-eyed priest in a black smock holding my crying mother. Did we go then into another room? Or was my father wheeled in to us? I don't know, I don't remember, but anyway here he is—my father, still and cool, on a metal table. The priest bends over him, thin lips moving in prayer. Some part of me wants to say the priest dips his two fingers in a squat, wide-mouthed glass bottle and traces a cross of oil on my father's forehead. Some part of me wants to say, in the fluorescent hospital lights, I can see the oil shine.

What I remember is my mother touching my father, her hands all over his chemical-yellow body: his stick arms and bloated face, his bald head and sunken chest. What I remember is the lot of us crying, even my grandfather. What I remember is it is all too much.

We leave. Or maybe my father is taken away. But somehow we are no longer where my father is, or where his body is, and we are collapsed into plastic hospital chairs. We are still weeping, though more quietly now, our hands useless and strange as wings in this too-bright room. We are there a few minutes or a few hours. I don't know. But whether he was wheeled away or was always in some other room, after those minutes or hours everyone gets up to see him one more time—even my little brother, whose sodden breath sounds now like small, sad bells—and I don't stand up, I don't rise from my chair to go with them. I don't go to see my father. Everyone else goes. I don't. I am sad and afraid, and they leave me this way.

Am I alone then? I seem to be alone, I see myself alone. Do they really leave me in that anonymous hospital room? Does the priest stay with me? Or one of the thin, busy nurses? I don't remember.

There is so much I do not remember.

And part of me wants to say, what of it? What does it mean, anyway, to remember? If a coyote clacks its yellow teeth in the night, if a cross of oil breaks and scatters the light, if I am alone or not alone— what does it matter? The light broke one way or another. That coyote must be dust. My father is in Montana still and is dust. And me? I am no longer that sad, roundheaded boy. No longer, if I ever was, scared and alone. Though I did not rise to see my father, I tell myself it does not matter.

Or do I, like a boy, pretend?

It goes like this: My wife and I are on our way home from visiting friends in Chicago. It is evening, our headlights beating back the dark along this flat, straight, Midwestern freeway. And I am resting in the passenger seat, my forehead on the cool window glass. Just out of Moline, I see beyond the fence line the quick blink and turn of yellow eyes—and like that I am a small boat drifting back on a muddy, snowmelt river of years; like that I am a brokenhearted, fatherless boy in the lonely-making distances of the interior; like that I want more than anything to rise and look again on my father. We leave and never leave. We grow up and never grow up. We grieve and grieve and grieve.

But sometimes, we remember, too, we turn and face that grief. Remembering is the opposite of pretending, it is the beginning of telling the truth to yourself about yourself. Yet I know—why did my grandfather, gentle cowboy that he was, have his hat on inside? Why the anointing then, when my father was already hours dead?—memory is never enough. Memory spins and skitters, winks in the dark. Like an oil slick, memory fails and rainbows the light. It is in the currents of story that the boy begins to understand. That the boy becomes a man. Becomes a better man. In story we learn to live like human beings in the dark houses of our bodies. For beyond anything we can do, we are alone in there. And we rightly spite that lonesome darkness. We reach out with what it is we have, fumble for the hand of the other—mother, brother, sister, lover, son—give to them our heart, our story.

There is one last thing I remember: My grandfather takes me in his hard arms. He pulls me up and out of my wool blankets and patch quilt. He sets me, gently, on the edge of the old army bunk I share with my brother. He tells me I must get dressed, but I am sleepy and do not want to wake and get dressed. I try to lie down and curl again beneath the covers. My grandfather does not shake or reprimand me. He simply takes me again in his arms. *Your father needs you*, he says. *You need to go to your father*.

I.

I want to believe

that if I get the story right

we will rise . . .

—NICK FLYNN

LAKE WATER

THE STORY GOES that it was the heat of August, that on a whim they'd packed their fishing gear and filled the cooler and drove north all day to meet my father's friend Jack Peters at Current Lake, a deep pool of the Missouri shadowed by the Little Rocky Mountains.

The whole place was crawling with rattlesnakes. Snakes sliding through the tall grass, snakes curled in the outhouse, snakes draped like question marks across the rocks. My mother walked everywhere with a long, stout stick to sling them off the footpath. My father carried a shovel and with it sliced the heads and rattles from those that twisted too near their tents. Jack Peters piled the dead snakes away from camp, for the flies, and to keep from scaring my five-year-old sister.

Despite the snakes, they caught a mess of trout that weekend, and swam in the afternoons, and drank a cooler of Rainier. They told stories late into the night, let the red-running embers of a pine fire play across their faces. They had a good time. And my mother tells me this was when I was conceived: this happy time, on a lake of clear water near the blue-black spines of mountains. She tells me they had long hoped for another child, a son, and she tells me, too, about the snakes.

But why? Why color the story with snakes? Why not simply say *mountain*, say *hope, lake, pine fire*?

I think it is because it makes the story better. More memorable, for sure. And truer, as well. To tell the story without snakes would be dishonest. Snakes complicate and foreshadow, shift like a crawling wind, hide in plain sight. And the high plains of Montana are thick with them: black and green water snakes ripple through irrigation ditches; sandy-scaled bull snakes, as big around as a fat man's arm, curl and doze on gravel roads; rattlesnakes shake their jangly tails off in the pear cactus and sagebrush.

My mother tells me the story of my origin—which, like all our stories, is shadowed, mythic, and particular—and so in her gladness and her grief she is obliged to speak of snakes.

My mother tells me the story of an August trip into the mountains. Of trout fried crisp in bacon grease. Of rattlers swimming down the rocks. It had been a long summer of chaff and dust and tractor grease. The lake water hurt their hands it was so cold.

SLOW BREATH

SOMETIMES IT IS okay, in the half-dark of an early midsummer morning, to climb out of bed, to leave your little brother slack-jawed and small and tangled in wool blankets, to pad quietly in white-footed pajamas down the hallway, through the bathroom's all-night odors of hard water and drying towels, and on into your parents' room.

It is breezy and cold, for they leave the window open at night, to breathe the good prairie air, and the floor is not carpeted but plain wood, the wallpaper peeling here and there. On your mother's dresser there are a few framed snapshots and a crucifix and maybe some bright necklaces and rings, a blouse or two. On your father's chest of drawers there is nothing save his watch and jackknife, his cracked snakeskin wallet. Yesterday's work jeans are draped across the foot of the bed, an old brown belt still strung through the loops. And the two of them: They are mountains of cream sheets, of musky warmth, slow breath, slow breath, slow breath.

You crawl—quietly, so very quietly—up onto the bed between them. Without a word, they make room for you, and you slide beneath

THE MOUNTAIN AND THE FATHERS

their scratchy sheets and pull the blankets up tight to your chin. Then you try to be as still as can be, as quiet as the sky. You wait and wait, nearly holding your breath with stillness—until slowly their bodies ease and their breaths slip and deepen, and you can relax, for they are asleep once more.

They need their sleep. They work hard. You know this. You understand that to be a boy here in this bent-back, make-do world is to be a shadow, off to the side of things and out of the way. Though here, for a sunrise span of minutes, you are the center of the unfolding universe.

Your father faces the wall, his broad back a sheer rising ridge, his white T-shirt stretched thin from thick shoulder to thick shoulder. With the tips of your fingers you feel the tight, black curls of his head, so unlike the dishwater mess you brush from your own eyes. Oh, it is something to be this close to him, to touch him, to breathe with your big-shouldered father. You breathe with him.

But you are more like your mother, you think, turning your round head to look at her soft, sleeping face. Not just your lank hair, but also the way she is facing you, not as a ridge but as hills and sweeping fields. That's how you feel, too, on the inside. You feel like plain old hills, a dry swath of buffalo grass, like you can turn your back to nothing, must face everything.

You aren't worried about this. Not yet, at least. Your father's hair didn't go dark and curl until he was in the army. You've heard the story many times, how he blames a shampoo his sister sent him from North Carolina. It'll be that way for you, too. You'll watch him. That's what you do: watch things, think about things. That's how you'll make your way through.

On the ceiling—it catches your eye, always—there is a pattern of cracks and twisting water damage. It looks like some shovel-headed, bent-nosed man. You don't like it, are scared of it, but the accident of that grim face holds you. You can't look away. You stare and stare, and the man stares back. You are about to squirm, to make a noise and wake your mother or your father or both of them—when the first morning meadowlark calls, and you can suddenly, thankfully look away.

You crane your neck to see out the window, to follow the bird's clear song: gauzy curtains lift and fill, the green-silver leaves of the plains cottonwood in the front yard tremble, ripple like water. And beyond, the very sky comes alive—all blue and slate and brightening smolder.

Here I am, you think. *In this bed between my strong father and my kind mother, in this good old house on the high plains of Montana. Here I am, just this boy.*

RAILROAD

I LIKE TO think I remember trains.

The Milwaukee Road railroad ran just a quarter mile south of our place. If you stepped out the screen door and stood on the cement steps, you could see the four-strand barbed-wire fence that marked our property, then Highway 12, and then running parallel to the highway the weedy gravel berm of the railroad. My grandfather often talked about riding the rails when he was looking for elevator work across eastern Montana. When my mother went off to college in Washington State, she took the Milwaukee Road the whole way. And whenever a train came rushing past, our old collie sheepdog Sam used to howl and howl.

The tracks were laid through our part of the country in 1908. Albert J. Earling was president of the Milwaukee Road then, and he wanted to get to the Pacific quicker and cheaper than anyone else, so he was willing to take a risk: Rather than follow a river valley through the cactus, sage, and bunchgrass prairies of Montana, as most of the previous transcontinental railroad lines had done, he cut across country, from the Yellowstone Valley at Forsyth over to the north bend of the

Musselshell River. Earling ran seventy-five miles of his railroad right through the driest, loneliest country in all Montana, a wide, wind-blown, light-shot high plain bounded on the north by the Missouri, on the south and east by the Yellowstone, and on the west by the Mus-selshell—yet the vast interior of this stretch of land is riverless. What springs there are burble with water so alkaline it is nearly poison; the few creeks run with rain and meltwater in the spring but quickly dry to dirt and gravel. They call this country the Big Dry, after the Big Dry River to the north, which Meriwether Lewis called "the most extraordinary river that I ever beheld. [I]t is as wide as the Missouri is at this place . . . and not containing a single drop of running water."

Crow, Assiniboine, Gros Ventre, and other natives once followed great herds of buffalo through the bunchgrass plains and badlands of the Big Dry, though all that came to a gruesome end in the winter of 1883–84, when the last of tens of thousands of free-roaming wild bison were on those very plains surrounded by commercial and government hunters and were slaughtered. A few years later, another hard winter brought down most of the big cattle barons; the stories have it that as the snow finally gave way in 1887, you could walk on the hides and bones of dead cows for miles without ever touching ground.

Then, for years, the Big Dry was wisely passed over and left alone. By 1908 it was all that was left of the wide-open West. Then came the Milwaukee Road. Then came passage of the Enlarged Homestead Act, designed to populate the arid lands, which allowed would-be farmers to claim double the usual allotment in the high plains and eastern Montana. Then came the hucksterism of rain following the plow, the pseudoscience of Hardy W. Campbell's *Soil Culture Manual*, a manifesto for dryland living that claimed adherence to certain till-age techniques and the purchase of a patented Campbell subsurface packer would make even a desert bloom. Then came a few discrep-ant seasons of full creeks and tall grass. Then came thousands and thousands of homesteaders, all with dreams of golden, heavy-headed wheat and a square half mile of Montana to call their own.

But then, of course, the rain quit falling, the creeks went dry—and the thin inch of living soil, held for millennia by the lacy, spidery roots of bunchgrass but plowed to a fine powder now by those hardworking homesteaders, blew away as so much dust. The populations of many eastern Montana counties peaked around 1918. And have been falling off ever since.

Those that stayed were too stubborn or too poor to move on. And so as neighbors left for Yakima and Tacoma, they opened up the fences. They scavenged old tractors and barn timber. They bought what abandoned land they could and took cheap leases on federal land. They gouged out irrigation ditches. They dug in, they scrounged, they made do. And it worked, for a time.

Along with his extended family and so many thousands of others, my great-grandfather came up from Oklahoma in the 1908 homestead rush. But he was a gambler and bootlegger and didn't leave a lick of land, or anything else, for my grandfather. As a young man, then, my grandfather cowboyed for wages. After he married, he took steady work managing grain elevators. Through it all, he saved. In 1954, he bought nine square miles of ranchland on the Big Dry, near Willow Creek, and some irrigated cropland along the Musselshell River, and then moved his family to the north bend of the river, to Melstone, Montana, a railroad town Earling named on the spot for a reporter in his entourage as he chugged on the completed railroad from water stop to water stop across the Big Dry and up the Musselshell Valley.

And even after the exodus of the 1920s, even after the privation of the dirty '30s, Melstone looked like a good bet. The grass on the Big Dry was thin, but it was grass, and cattle need room to roam. Most years the river ran all through August, which kept the county ditch full and the farmland green. To the south of the river were the box canyons and jack pines of the Bull Mountains, where a truckload of good furnace coal could be had for cheap. When my parents moved back to the Big Dry in '73, the trains came whistling by morning, noon, and night.

I like to think I remember trains.

Sam shivering on the step, howling low and loud as the coal cars barrel down the tracks. But even for the way I can see Sam's black head thrown back, I'm almost sure I don't remember. I think instead I remember my grandfather's stories and my mother's stories, and the stories of the old men drinking coffee at the Lazy JC Drug and Hardware Store. I think in the swirl of years those stories have slipped and mixed with memory. To be honest, I don't even think I remember the tracks, as I have heard how the railroad company came by not long after the trains quit running in 1980, pulling up the rails and ties for salvage—yet I can see them, in my mind's eye, burnished and narrowing into the Bull Mountains.

For years after the tracks came up, folks scavenged the one thing the company left: railroad spikes, the iron proof of that lost civilization. My brother and sister and I had a collection in the log cabin, an old homesteader's shack behind the house that we used as a playhouse, and I had a number of the best ones, solid and not too rusty, in my room. With the trains gone, Sam took to howling at the fat B-52s that boomed over us all hours of the day. They were on bombing runs, pretending the abandoned distances of eastern Montana were some far Russian plain. In only the span of one man's lifetime—my grandfather was born in a sod shanty near Billings in 1914 and was still riding the prairie for strays and fixing fence when the Berlin Wall came down some seventy-five years later—the Big Dry and the lower Musselshell River country had gone from dream to dream: I don't remember passenger trains, I remember bombers: immense and untouchable, gone in a thudding clap of thunder.

We often walked the old railroad bed, my sister collecting agates to run through her polisher, my brother and I chewing grass stems and watching for spikes and bones, my mother telling us stories as we ambled east toward Lee's slough or west toward the messy stand of cottonwoods and willows along the banks of the county ditch. When we were older, we were allowed to walk the tracks by ourselves— maybe my sister taking us down to the slough to swim or my brother and I crouching through the horseweeds between the tracks and the highway, pretending we were Custer's Crow scouts.

Older yet, and I put my slingshot, a book, and a ham-and-butter sandwich in my backpack and took off for Damon Lear's house. Damon was my age and his folks owned the place just to the west of us. Though the trip was only a couple of miles, it felt a mountain of time. I loved those enormous afternoons, the stink of sage in the hot wind, the feeling of being on my way. Even after Damon's grandparents sold the place and his father had to go work for another man, I walked the railroad bed. Sometimes I would find eagle feathers and old beer cans with pop-tops. Sometimes I would find the body of a deer or house cat that had been hit on the highway and with its last strength pulled itself into the bar ditch, a string of iridescent flies sipping at its velvet nose, its slack mouth. Sometimes I sat right down in the ashy gravel.

I had nowhere to go.

I watched the highway, tallied what traffic there was that day: farmer in a rattling Ford, trucker barreling along, maybe a bright sports car or low-bellied sedan from who knows where. It astonished me that this highway could still carry a body to Spokane or Seattle, Rapid City or Minneapolis. It almost didn't seem possible. I'm not sure I believed you could get from here to there.

Here, where they tore the tracks from beneath us, where the B-52s boomed and vanished above us.

Two Fragments from My Grandfather's Body

COYOTE BAIT

I TOUCH MY grandfather's hand, trace the seam of scar that runs his palm from wrist to pinky. The mark is ragged, loud and white against his sun-dark skin. Beneath, the flesh is ridged and drawn, hard to the touch. The cyanide shell, shot from a powdered coyote getter, practically tore his hand in half.

I have heard the story many times: He's setting the coyote getter near a sheep kill along the north bank of Willow Creek when it accidentally fires, and there's blood and black poison all over his hands and his boots, blood splashing in the dust, and his daughter, my mother, just a skinny kid of thirteen, is screaming. He's calm. He says, "Swede"—short for sweetheart, what he always calls his only daughter—"just settle down and drive. Drive me on into town now, Swede." She listens, he lives, and I know my grandfather was lucky or strong. For though I am young, maybe five or six, I have seen sheep drop with a bullet to the ear, the belly laid open, what was inside laid out, and I know there is death somewhere back of this scar.

My grandfather grins at me, suddenly wraps his hand around my finger like a vise. His gray eyes, not stone but blue-silver, like sage, light as he twists my arm up and around and behind my back. He says it'll take more than a bit of coyote bait to put this old boy under, and holds for a second longer—then lets go.

I rub my arm, careful to look down so he does not see my watery blue eyes. He's always giving me Indian burns, putting me in head locks, pinching the backs of my arms—always a little too hard— but I love him anyway, love him because the barrel-chested fathers of my friends and the old men drinking coffee at the Lazy JC and Donny Kicker who runs the sawmill across the highway all look at me strangely. I talk more than a child should and have been put up in the higher grades for math and reading at school, and both my father and my mother went to college. But this one man, uneducated and burly as any of them, my grandfather—whose crib was a boot box on a woodstove, who sat on the jug when his daddy ran whiskey, who's broke a thousand horses and been struck by lightning twice—does not care. He grins and tosses me into the world of scars and bod- ies, the world of cyanide shells and sheep kills, the world of his dark hands. There is the craggy bark of the cottonwood in front of the house, the soft brown shag on the front room floor, and my grandfa- ther's hands, tough as worked leather.

"Come on, pardner," he says, clapping me hard on the back. "Let's go get some grub."

80 PROOF

THEY ARE men in their prime—rifles slung across broad backs, grinning winks at wives and children, antelope blood all over blue jeans. The men, my father and three of his college buddies, say my brother and I, at six and eight, are too young for the hunt—"You'll have to ride with your grandfather." I am indignant, sure that my successful summer of prairie dog hunting with the old .22 caliber bolt-action Winchester qualifies me to ride with them, and I am stunned that my grandfather, an expert tracker and the best rifle shot in the county behind Buster Knapp, stands for what amounts to a day of babysitting. But, despite my protests, we three climb into Old Blue, my grandfather's flatbed Ford, and follow the men past Melstone and north up the Mosby Road and out to my grandfather's dryland ranch, out onto the snapping bunchgrass and sage of the Big Dry.

My grandfather drives slowly across the hills and plains of eastern Montana, across these miles of prairie he calls his, and he tells us stories. Like the one about skinning squirrels for stew in the dirty '30s, or the coyote he once shot at nearly four hundred yards running. He drives on and tells us that wild game is fine meat cooked on the stove with plenty of pepper, and even better over a pine fire. With a flick of his wrist, he slips his glasses off his face so he can clearly see the prairie. Since he was very young he has been farsighted, and now, somewhere in the distance, he spots a buck antelope with a freak horn that swings back at the tip instead of forward. He hands us the binoculars so we, his grandsons with the nearsightedness of their bookish mother, can take a look. And sometime after lunch, as the sun swings to the west, he says that he doesn't have it in him anymore, that he's done hunting, that he believes he'll leave off the killing.

I half listen, angry and uncaring, hoping someone will soon rectify the injustice done to me today. No one seems to notice. We follow the men as they fill their tags in turn, and when night falls we follow them to the camp house, where my grandfather and father stay during shearing or branding or whenever work won't let them get back to the river. It is cold and inky dark outside, clouds obscuring the stars, but the cabin is oven warm and lit with the smoky light of oil lamps. My brother and I get a bottle of root beer apiece and are told to sit at the table, to pet the barn cat, to watch out for the cracking heat of the wood stove. The men do not let my grandfather sit with us. They crowd around him, call him "Mr. Maxwell." They nearly trip over themselves to tell him about the particulars of each of their kill shots. They roll him a cigarette. They offer him a beer. He waves off both, saying, "I quit for the boys' grandmother" and "I don't drink nothing if it ain't eighty proof." They all laugh, light up, and ask for stories.

My grandfather tilts his battered gray cowboy hat back on his bald head and tells them about skinning those same squirrels for stew, and even before he finishes explaining the particulars of the old .22 caliber bolt-action Winchester he hunted with, my brother and I are asleep.

Later, I half wake as someone carries me out to the truck. The road home is dirt and gravel and rocks me in and out of dreams. I hear my grandfather. I try hard to pull myself from sleep. I want to listen now. Again I see the light in their eyes, the eyes of grown men, at his stories. As if they were asking a blessing.

But sleep pulls me back, and a soft light grows on the far prairie, and there are great herds of antelope, and I am walking through them, touching their hard and ragged horns.

Out West, Part One

OUT ON THE Big Dry, we had to kill to live:

Come October, we'd herd a yearling lamb into the west pen, throw it some good flakes of alfalfa hay. It'd be grass-fat by then, nearly tame—just chewing, and looking around, and chewing. My father, his black hair bright and wild in the early winter light, would put the rifle barrel in its soft ear and pull the trigger. We were nearly two hours away from the nearest city supermarket. And even if we were closer, we couldn't afford it. We ate lamb all winter—lamb chops and leg of lamb and lamb stew with garden peas my mother canned. All kinds of lamb. We scooted our chairs up to the kitchen table, and we said our grace, and we ate. We talked of the day, of the many days that brought us this meal—lamb roast with potatoes and onions, slices of bread pan-fried in salt and lamb fat, a plate of radishes and garden carrots—and the many days this root and grain and meat would give us. Each day we celebrated three squares this very way, save Sunday, of course, when dinner wasn't until two or three in the afternoon, since pulling a fryer out of the freezer was always quite a to-do.

Butchering chickens, too, was an all-day affair, a late-summer festival of sorts, a kind of prairie celebration. We put on our old jeans and stained snap shirts and ate a big breakfast of hamburger steak, eggs, and potatoes. My mother and grandmother set up aluminum basins of hot water for the plucking. My father and grandfather sharpened knives and hatchets. And when everything was finally ready, they sent us children into the coop.

A moment later, we scrambled out slicked with shit and feathers, holding squawking hens to our heaving chests. We gave those orange and brown and piebald hens over to my father or my grandfather, whoever happened to be kneeling behind the pine stump that day, and one by one they stretched the hens out on the stump and stroked their necks until they calmed and then brought the hatchet down hard. They gave them back to us—still flapping and jerking, blood suddenly everywhere—by their bony feet.

There'd be a line of us, happy children holding headless chickens upside down, blood running out and all over the dust.

I REMEMBER my grandfather standing above me, his breath steaming out of him. He was telling me to take my knife and cut the throat of the first antelope I had ever shot. I was twelve years old and confused.

Some hours ago and some four hundred yards up the hill, I lay down in the scalloped dirt and wind-crusted snow and snugged the stock of my .243 Winchester up to my right shoulder. Then, I waited. Maybe forty minutes, maybe an hour, maybe two. Hard to tell. The sun was a white hole in the cold, blue sky. The wind bit at the wet of my eyes. I could feel the land pressing up against me, as if buoying me against the wind and the sky.

I scanned the bright flats before me. Before he limped away, my grandfather had told me he thought a herd of antelope might have bedded down north of here; he thought he might get upwind of them and push them my way. And, indeed, from the sage and shadow of the coulee, an antelope stepped, then another, then two and three, and some dozen or more. On willow-thin limbs they stepped slowly, munching at the yellow tufts of grass ridging the snow. A buck stopped and turned.

There. Right there, back of his foreleg, that was the small pocket where I would put a bullet to still his heart. I let the crosshairs drift over him. I breathed and squeezed the trigger. The explosion was terrific. I didn't see the buck fall, wasn't even sure I hit him, but the herd bolted, and I scrambled up anyway and slid the rifle's safety on and ran, my breath coming hard and cold.

And now I was kneeling. I had no idea it would be like this.

This thing laid out on the snow before me—as if leaping, as if in a last memory of leaping—was so fine and beautiful. It's true that my shot was beautiful too—nearly four hundred yards and clean through the heart—and between these two beauties it seemed like it all ought to be over, it seemed like I should be done; I was looking to my grandfather for help, for release from this duty—but he shook his head. The hunt is about the hunt, but even more than that it is about sustenance, about the life this antelope took from the land, the life we would take from this antelope. I turned back to the buck, took up my eight-inch bone-handled knife—a Christmas gift from the year before—and eased the bright blade through the skin of the buck's neck and the hollow beneath.

There is so much blood in a thing.

After I gutted him and packed him up the ridge and loaded him into the bed of the pickup, I stood in the clear, cold light of morning, marveling at my blood-crusted jeans, my still blood-wet hands. All winter, I knew, we'd eat breakfasts of antelope steak and fried eggs, earthy-tasting antelope sausage mixed into cream gravy and poured over toast come dinner. My father was years dead by then, and my mother came home from work each day tired in the dark. This blood, I thought, will get us through.

My grandfather broke my reverie. He took me by the shoulders, told me I had done a good, hard thing and done it well. And he told me to be careful that it always remained a hard thing to do. "Easy isn't any good," he said. "If it ever gets easy, quit."

BONE

BUT LET ME say this too: Even so, I was a boy.

Morning's dandelion light spilling over us, my brother and I sprint—screen door banging, arms pumping, little legs cranking as fast as they can—into the shelterbelt west of the house. Here, in this wonderfully overgrown acre, where the crazy-making plains wind breaks for a moment and scatters, are white-barked birch, slender spruce, messy cottonwood, bright-fruited chokecherry, and thorny Russian olive. Here, we are mountain men, maybe Colter and Bridger, down to our last sack of powder and hiding a cache of beaver pelts along the rain-fat river that is the dry irrigation ditch. Here, we are silent Lakota, slipping over the Wolf Mountains, catching Custer unaware. Here, we are wizards, soldiers, superheroes, greasers—two lost boys lolling in the tall grass, watching on a summer afternoon immense, anvil-headed clouds slide through the wide Montana sky, wondering about this and that and the world beyond the four-strand fence ringing the far field.

Lunch is a quick picnic of BLTs and root beer floats our mother serves on the front porch. After, we strip off our shirts and spray each other with the garden hose. Then we crawl up onto the roof of the log cabin, the old homesteader's shack slouched in the far southwest corner of the shelterbelt, and lie down on the sizzling tin and bake our naked backs and bellies in the summer sun. Now and then we stand and unzip and piss great arcs out into the trees. Finally, our skin baked reddish brown, we climb down, sit in the musky shade inside the dirt-floored cabin and catalogue our treasures. For wherever we go—skipping along the irrigation ditches, out into the fields, down to the river, walking the old railroad bed—we gather and bring back treasure: mother-of-pearl mussel shells, rusted railroad spikes, bits of green and purple glass left by hard-luck homesteaders and years ago plowed under, the hollow bones of a hawk. Always, we gather bones. We have a whole collection, though we didn't start it and don't know who did. It has just always been here, on the back shelf and spilling below the back shelf, this bone shrine: here the airy, palm-sized skull of prairie dog; there the squat, thick leg bones of black bear. We pick them up in our pink hands and warm them, and they take on what life we give them. We dream them back into muscle and skin, fur and claw. We consider this particular bear, this certain sharp-faced coyote. We consider then the thin bones beneath our own sunburnt skin, hope they too can as be as lovely, last so long.

We feel a kinship and responsibility to bones.

Finally, the crickets and frogs starting up their racket, breaking our reverie, we run dirty and sun-washed and shoeless and starving back into the house, where dinner is fried antelope chops and boiled potatoes. Afterward, we all sit in the front room: my mother in her rocking chair reading *Newsweek*, my sister painting her nails on the couch, and laid out on the soft brown shag my brother and I building out of Legos intricate sailing ships and airplanes and space-crafts to Andromeda. Before bed, we climb onto the piano bench and place our various Lego creations up on the dusty piano top, near the photos of our dead father—here, he is in his army uniform; here, he wears lamb-chop sideburns and holds our mother at the waist; here, the magpie he tamed perches on his arm—and then clamber down and brush our teeth and crawl under sheets and wool blankets and patch quilts, and long into the night my brother and I whisper stories to one another—stories we crib from the books we read, from our tall-tale grandfather, from the radio and the television, from the old men drinking coffee at the Lazy JC, from waking dreams and sleepy visions. Our stories are as real as anything we have done that day. We tell each other story after story, until sleep lifts us softly from ourselves.

And to the rich-sour smells of antelope sausage and buttermilk hotcakes, the snap of hot grease, we wake. We step now, sleepily, from our bedroom—which is really just the dead end of the hallway, as our house, with its odd seams and uneven ceilings and hollow walls, was years ago scavenged and hammered together from the husks and scraps of some half-dozen abandoned homesteaders' shacks—and we sit up at the table to eat our dish of canned fruit and wait for a sausage and pile of cakes, the warm plains wind slipping in around the cracked dining room window.

And still tired from yesterday's ranch work but cooking breakfast for us anyway, my mother is mother and father and God, and my sister with her makeup and Jon Bon Jovi–in-a-leather-jacket poster is a teenager, and my sleepy-eyed brother is a boy, and I am a boy: towheaded and loved, delighted by everything, confused by everything, growing right out of my hand-me-down blue jeans and hungry for the new day.

My Mother's Story,
Part One

IT IS MAY of 1970. She is twenty-nine and slender, red-blond hair hanging to her waist. She has graduated from college, worked, traveled from Nome, Alaska, to New York City. She lives now in the little city of Billings, Montana, and every time they rotate shows at the art museum she's there opening night. She knows the janitors at the public library by name. She's still mourning Bobby Kennedy and Dr. King. She cried when she found out Nixon had troops in Cambodia. Just last year she bought a car, her first, a little white Chevelle. She only smokes when someone offers.

Each morning at St. Patrick's, she lights three candles, one each for hope, faith, and love. In the evening, she goes downtown with her friends, and they all drop their nickels in the jukebox for Buffy St. Marie and Dylan's early stuff, anything by Joan Baez. They talk for hours. They're intelligent, passionate. They're all students and teachers and social workers dedicated to the hard slog of change. They believe peace can happen, if they work hard enough, if they all lose themselves in that greater good. Then my mother orders another drink and leans in, tells her friends about skinny-dipping in the Bering Sea, white ice dazzling her white skin. They laugh out loud, brush their long hair from their eyes.

Yet even for it all—her job, that good café—she thinks about leaving. She's got friends in Minneapolis, New York State, loves Montreal; she misses seeing every day something wonderful and new. But then there are her parents, living still two hours north of Billings, working that dusty ranch out on the Big Dry. Though in her twenty-nine years she's never done what they expected, she's felt bad about it every time. She has some odd, inborn sense of responsibility. Not that the ranch would ever come to her. She's a woman, still single.

You're getting older, her mother tells her on the phone.

Yes, she says, and happily. She left home at seventeen, had seen New York by twenty-four. Each year, she thinks, a little older, a little more myself.

Lawrence, her younger brother, calls from Missoula. He's in his last year at the University of Montana and getting married in July. He tells her he could use some help getting things ready for the wedding. So, over Memorial Day, she jumps in her Chevelle and drives clear across the state. She picks up a bearded hitchhiker out of Belgrade. Together, they pray for the students killed at Kent State, for all the soldiers ordered to do the killing.

Lawrence, his hair longer than ever, meets her at his apartment door. He brushes beer cans and newspapers off the couch so she can sit. He rambles on about his wife-to-be, his slender hands moving through the air—but he stops, suddenly, and takes his glasses off. He leans forward, looks at her, tells her he knows someone she has to meet. His name's Walt. He's seen her picture. He's interested. She's not interested. She's embarrassed, aggravated. Lawrence should know she's not looking. Her job doesn't leave her any time; there are just too many needy families out there. Besides, this Walt is nearly three years younger than she is—and she only dates older men. They're more mature, she says, and considerate. But Lawrence insists.

Walt's dressed in pressed slacks and a collared shirt. His hair is deep black, not long but thick and wavy. He wears sideburns, his shoulders straight as boards, and his chest tapers to trim hips. They walk downtown in the sunset shadows of the mountains, the lilacs just beginning to blossom. They wait in line at the movie house and see M*A*S*H. He laughs easy and often. They go for a drink afterward. He knows the bartenders, orders beer for them both. He tells her he likes her name, Olive. It sounds Southern, reminds him of home. Home is North Carolina, a farm along the bottomlands. He tells her about mornings when fog moved in off the cypress swamp and mixed with the heady smell of curing tobacco, when you could drink dew from the magnolia leaves. But after his time in the army, testing chemicals and all kinds of things down in Panama, he wanted to keep moving, go west and take it all in. A buddy in his unit said there was good fishing near Missoula, so he applied to the university. He'll graduate with a degree in forestry this December. Afterward? He isn't sure. All he knows is he's fallen in love with the West, with Montana, the plains pouring east off the front, the rocky rumple of mountains—and especially Glacier Park. He's worked there the last three summers, is going to do it again. He invites her to visit him. He'll take her into the backcountry, they'll ride horses through cool forests of fir and cedar, he'll show her the best streams to fish. He tells her he'll write her, says she is as pretty as her picture.

She likes the way he talks but doesn't believe a word he says.

The first letter arrives three days after she gets back to Billings.

It's Thursday, nearly suppertime, and she's tired. She's thinking that the state is broke and takes it out on children, that too many of the families she works with have been pushed right to the edge—not enough money for rent and less for the doctor. All these places are so sad: just brick apartments, crying babies, the stink of urine and smoke. She's upset as well about the conservative, book-banning ignorance all around—and Nixon, God that Nixon. She wonders why she doesn't leave, go back to New York City, maybe down to California, travel again, just drive and drive and take a look at things, curl up at night in the backseat of the Chevelle and read by starlight.

But this letter is something else—polite and charming, direct. He says he's coming over to the east side of the state next week with his friend, Jack Peters, to visit Jack's parents before they both go to work up in Glacier for the summer. He'll take her dancing, if she doesn't mind, when he gets in on Tuesday.

She feels dizzy, flushed. She can't seem to make it stop. He was rather handsome.

Billings is her town, the biggest and fastest-growing in the state, and she wants to impress him, so she takes him to that place downtown where the house band plays jazz and the drinks come in crystal glasses. He fidgets with his napkin, looks around too much. She asks if he'd like to go somewhere else. He stands right up, says, Yes. Please.

She takes his hand, leads him out. They walk down First Avenue, the sweet manure stench of the public auction yards and the sulfury belch of the sugar beet refineries perfuming the night. When they pass some ramshackle honky-tonk called Bar 17, he stops and smiles, swings wide the wooden doors.

They dance the Texas swing. They sweat and drink cold bottles of Rainier beer. She likes how he moves, takes the lead so easily. Over the whine of the fiddle, the lilting steel guitar, he leans in close and tells her she's beautiful. She blushes, and the band starts into an old Carter Family ballad, "When the Roses Bloom Again." She tells him she heard Johnny Cash sing this one at the state fair last year. He says it's one of his favorites. They stay on the dance floor. They're close, very close, moving slow. She is in his arms.

Oh, and this, this too:

He's working at the park. He knows someone who flies a charter plane between Billings and Great Falls and gets her a seat sometime in late June. She flies into the Great Falls airport, just a tin hangar out on the plains, and he and Jack pick her up wearing cowboy hats, jeans, and boots. They've been riding trail, and she can smell the musk of horse on them. He reminds her of her cowboy father coming in from a day on the ranch—but then he smiles and the thought dissolves in waves.

That night they drink Kessler Beer and bourbon whiskey straight from the bottle at the Izaak Walton Inn, where the only other woman at the bar is an old blood Indian everyone calls Mother. The next day, Jack wakes up just to go back to bed. So they ride through the mountains, just the two of them, cool wind across their faces. They pick wild strawberries, cook brook trout in bacon grease over a pine fire, sleep in a wash of stars.

And each weekend after, they cannot help themselves. One of them gets a lift with a friend or hitchhikes to the other. She feels electric Friday evening, in a stranger's car, music loud, the windows down, the sun falling red and wild, as they rush by Grass Range and Great Falls and on up past Dutton—and she sees the wheat fields, sees the green wheat pale, and turn gold, and finally deeper gold.

Then, summer's over. He has to study for his comprehensives. They write letter after letter, so many letters. After graduation, he drinks all night with Jack, and then flies back to North Carolina. She marks off the days with a stubby pencil. He's gone a few weeks that seem to her years.

Finally: January 1971, snow on the streets of Billings, she gets a call: He says he's got a full-time job with the Forest Service, in Seattle, and he starts in two weeks. Will she come with him? Will she marry him?

The world collapses. It is only the two of them. War and poverty and her friends and all the books she's read and all the places she meant to travel and the great distances of Montana no longer matter—because he is asking her to marry him.

31

She wears her mother's dress. He's bought a secondhand suit that he can wear to work next week as well. Her parents are there, her father in his wide-brimmed hat and boots, and her brother Lawrence. No one from his family makes it up, but his mother sends her his favorite biscuit recipe. The priest says the greatest of these is love, and Jack Peters sneaks liters of two-dollar champagne into the church basement in emptied soda bottles.

Walt and Olive, husband and wife, drive off after the reception in their white Chevelle. They're headed farther west. His foot is heavy on the gas, the wind is icy cold—but they are fast and warm. He sings some Gordon Lightfoot songs, some Johnny Cash songs. She claps and laughs. They drive on through moonlight and snow-covered mountains and the wide and darkening sky.

She likes Seattle, works in a library, reads, listens to lectures. She thinks she could live here—but he doesn't. He hates the traffic, the freeways, the gray rag of cloud where the blue sky should be.

After just six months, he requests a transfer to the mountains of Durango, Colorado, where she finds work at a hospital and finds out she's pregnant as well. It's a girl. He hammers together a playpen and makes plans to pack his little daughter all over the mountain trails of the four corners. She learns to cook and sew. She makes biscuits and potato pancakes and all his favorites. She spends hours on intricate pink dresses, nurses their daughter as the nights get hot, the soap smell of cactus flowers lifting in the wind. She even starts a garden, though she never harvests it.

They're eating enchiladas and drinking cold beer at a ramshackle place just out of town. He takes a long swig and tells her he can't stand it any longer. With the promotion, he sits at a desk all day long and looks at maps. He's lucky if he gets two days in the mountains all month. He pauses, then looks her in the eye and tells her he's been talking with her father—struck a deal in fact. He's found a way to be out on the land every day: Her father's agreed to split his place back in Montana. He's going to give them a good price for the irrigated farm along the river, and then they'll have the first crack at the pasture on the Big Dry when her father retires.

She is surprised. She loves Colorado. She doesn't know what to say. She finishes her enchiladas.

They drive out of Durango as the leaves of the aspens begin to yellow, Wyoming takes forever, and then they finally meet the Musselshell River out of Roundup. They turn off Highway 12 and down the gravel road. Her parents greet them from the porch. Her father tells them that they get the main house, winks—says they'll need it for all the kids, that he'll build a smaller grandpa-and-grandma-sized house just down the road.

Walt's ecstatic, rough and joyful in his new work. He wakes at dawn each day to haul lumber for the new corrals he's planned. Olive packs their squalling daughter in her arms, paces all day the white and yellow lino-leum—the cracks just beginning to show here and there. They live far north even of Billings and her old friends, in a county with only a single paved road laid right through its heart, out in the great and perfect isola-tion of the Montana plains.

But she says they're happy, insists that they are happy—farming their land, making a go of it, their faces chapped of prairie wind. He gets along well with her father, works hard all week, drinks at the Sportsman Bar on Fri-day night. She puts in another garden, nearly two acres. Her tomatoes grow like weeds, and her cucumbers are dazzling quartered and splashed with salt. In the heat of August they curl up together on the foldout couch in the cool basement and listen to Lightfoot records on their hi-fi.

The years are wet and good. The wheat sells, the barley sells, the sheep get fat. He's elected to the school board and the Musselshell County Irri-gation Association. She runs the Altar Society at Our Lady of Mercy.

They are respected all down the valley. They try for another child. They want a boy. The years go by with nothing. Still, they try—because they have faith, and they have faith, and in the late fall of '77 she finds out she's pregnant again.

The sun spills into their room, and she wakes to pain. They drop their daughter off at her parents' place and drive to Billings. The Chevelle runs strong. It is early May of 1978. The snow packed deep on the mountains this last winter and the rains have come all spring, the grass already tall and thick, the mud-brown Musselshell River brimming and slapping at its banks.

At the hospital he won't take no for an answer. He scrubs up, puts on a white coat, follows the nervous young doctor into the delivery room. She is so happy he is there. She sweats and screams. She holds on to him. She holds on to him. There is a gush of blood, and the doctor takes me from her and hands me to him.

He holds me first.

My mother tells me, always, that he holds me first. Tells me he is covered in blood, her blood and my blood, and he leans down to her and whispers, "We got our boy."

She stays in the hospital for three more days, but he can't take that much time. He must get back to irrigate. He kisses her, drives home by moonlight, a Lightfoot tune on his lips.

I see him now walking the ditch bank, shovel over his shoulder. There is the weedy stink of alfalfa and the rich smell of mud, the far call of a coyote and a second coyote yipping back across the hills. The half-moon is white and wide among the pinprick stars. He comes to the canvas dam and sinks his shovel in the ditch bank. He kneels, rolls up his sleeves and reaches into

34

the water, grabs the wooden stake across the top of the dam and pulls. With a muddy suck the canvas slips and lifts, and water rushes on down the ditch, filling the next dam, where it will flood the next dike, where it will bring forth from this dryland sweet grass and leafy alfalfa.

And now he rises, holding his dripping hands out from him. The moon is white and pale, not yet full, but so bright his wet arms seem to shine with some light inside them, a bright bone-light. He is thinking, Joe, just Joe, like that quarterback from Notre Dame with the crackerjack of an arm. And Robert, like my father.

He is thinking about tromping back along the ditch bank.

He is thinking about days spent fixing machinery, plowing land, irrigating fields with his son beside him.

He is thinking about faith, hope, and love. How it is hope that swallows him whole, hope and moonlight all around.

GRASS

IN THE PHOTOGRAPH, my mother holds my brother on her right hip. He is a chubby toddler, with a tuft of downy hair so blond it's white, and he is wearing my sister's hand-me-down pink pajamas. My mother's hair has reddened, has grown long again and parts around her face, is taken a bit in what small wind there must have been that day. Behind her is the stubby plains cedar my father dug up in the Bull Mountains and planted in the yard. There are sheets of plastic stapled over the windows, which means the photograph, bright as it is, was probably taken on some unseasonably warm, late winter day.

My mother does not look old, but she does not look young either. There are crow's feet at the corners of her eyes, and her face is somewhat drawn. She is handsome now, not slender but thin. She leans into my father and smiles into the camera, into the wind and sun. My sister is to the right of my mother, in front of my father, and she looks in this photograph very much like him—the same wide face and high cheekbones and thin line of smile. Like my mother, though, her hair has gone all tawny and gold.

The clear center here is my father. He is as big as all the rest of us. A head taller than my mother, wide as my mother and sister together. The only thing that bests my father is the house behind him—part of a window, the porch, the screen door, which is bright and silver and must be new—and between the cedar and the house, the sky.

My father wears a blue work shirt, the collar open, a pen and pad of paper in his left front pocket. His chin is small and knobbed—is weak, like mine—though his face thickens then and is ruddy and dark from days working in the sun. His mustache and cropped curls shine blue-black. I imagine my grandfather is the one taking the picture, as this is just the way he would have set it up, moved us around, framing my father there in the center of us. It is a well-shot photo, though my father's eyes are nearly closed. It is this way in all the pictures I have of him healthy: He smiles his eyes closed.

And he holds me. His left arm is around me as I perch on the top rail of the wooden fence. I am wearing overalls and a blue undershirt, an old straw cowboy hat. I am barefoot. In my right hand I grip the barrel of a toy six-gun. My left hand is on my father's left hand, the one tucked around my middle. It is almost as if we'd posed it: one hand small and tender, the other large and sure. But here the picture is flawed, for I am not facing the camera. I look out of the corner of the photograph. I am maybe three or four. I do not remember the photo and do not know what it is I am looking at. Maybe a barn cat come out to soak up the sun. Maybe Sam, our sheepdog, patiently waiting for his work. Maybe the grass, the light and shadow in the late-winter grass.

I don't know. I know at least this once my father holds me.

II.

Or are you just looking

for another father?

How many fathers does

one boy need?

—E.L. DOCTOROW

KEITH NELSON

WHAT WE ARE having for dinner tonight are cheeseburgers and Oreo cookies, and we are eating this dinner—gnashing our still-bloody burgers, crumbling cookie after cookie, washing it all down with big, breathless glugs of root beer—on the lone piece of furniture in Keith Nelson's front room, a faded yellow couch. This is not what we ought to be eating for dinner, and this is not where we are supposed to be eating our dinner either. What's more, we are definitely not supposed to be eating cheeseburgers and cookies in the living room—sitting cross-legged on the couch, plates held just beneath our smeary chins—while watching John Wayne westerns, which is of course what we are doing, switching to the next video cassette just as soon as the sun sets over the settlers and the cowboy tips his hat and rides away.

My older sister is staying the night with a friend from school. At four and five, my brother and I are too young for school, too young to have friends, which is why we are staying at Keith Nelson's house. Our father dropped us off here earlier this evening, before pulling on his good brown suit and straightening his bolo tie and taking our mother dancing at a fancy hotel in Billings. Keith's house sits across the river from ours, in the sloped shadows of the Bull Mountains. It is low-slung and ramshackle and more than a bit messy, though none of that matters. Keith is a bachelor. He is maybe twenty-four or twenty-five and skinny as a fence post. He wears brown cowboy boots, blue jeans, a white T-shirt. He feathers his dark hair back behind his ears. Keith is, anyone can see it, straight handsome—which, along with his shy, ungainly way, makes him all the more different from the usual toothless, loud-mouthed, bulb-nosed farmers who work these plains. We have in fact never even been told to call him "Sir" or "Mr. Nelson." He has always been "Keith Nelson," who is young and awkward and handsome and lives alone across the river, or just "Keith," who my father has taken under his wing and teases but treats kindly—like an apprentice of sorts, or a son.

"As many cheeseburgers as you can eat," Keith says, standing in the doorway between the front room and the kitchen, having to lean down a bit, because he is so tall, though when he sees us turn to look at him, he chuckles and looks away, as if even here in his own house he is somehow embarrassed. He says nothing about the ketchup spatters, nothing about the crumbs—he just smiles and chuckles and ducks his head like he does, his big Adam's apple ducking and bobbing too, and turns back to the kitchen, where in a moment we hear the next round of meat sizzle and pop on the skillet. My brother and I grin at each other, our round faces shining with grease.

We grin because Keith doesn't know what he's doing, though he is trying, has been trying mightily all evening, to act like he knows. We love Keith for both his ignorance and his aspiration—love that he has never spoken with a child and so speaks to us as if we are adults, love that we'll be able to convince him to let us stay up past midnight and eat ice cream right out of the bucket. We love, too, that he would do this at all—take us into his house and feed us and turn down for us the covers of the big musty bed that used to be his parents'—because it means he respects our father. He is doing this, and trying to do it right, because we are our father's sons. There is no other reason. We could have been dropped off with the Bergins or the Lears or some other neighbors with a passel of kids. But we sit here instead, two young boys in an awkward and lonely man's house, two young boys out on the far and unforgiving plains of the country, and we are safe, are as happy as can be—even here, we are fathered.

After dinner, we help Keith with the evening chores. We toss alfalfa hay to the sheep, gather warm eggs from beneath the bantam hens, fill the horse trough. Then come in and wash up. My brother and I change into our white-footed pajamas and run and slide across the wooden floor and leap up onto the couch. Keith warms a last round of cheeseburgers in the oven and brings them out on a big tin plate. I grab one and my brother grabs one, and we slather them with ketchup. Keith sits down too, right between us, and grabs the last burger for himself, and together we watch the cowboys ride at a gallop up and over the ridge.

PA PETERS

HIS PALSIED HANDS shiver as he twists the fishing line one, two, three, four times around—then threads it through. He pulls the tangle of line tight and drops the blue-silver lure. It swings between us. "That's a fisherman's knot," Pa Peters tells me, and chuckles and pushes his thick glasses up the bridge of his bent nose. "That's how you do it."

I take my pole from Pa and thank him and step into the icy lake water and wade out to a dark, flat-topped rock. I cast, then reel in my line, cast and reel, again and again—and the sun arcs slowly over and down and behind the granite maw of the Beartooth Mountains. Finally, the light long and shadows longer, I lay my pole down and sit cross-legged on my rock and watch Pa Peters.

He is old, easily the oldest person I know. He shakes and cannot hear things, his hair is salt white. I don't think he's related to us by blood, but I am to call him "Pa"—do not even know his given name—because my father loves Pa Peters as if he were his own father: They fish together. In college, my father and Pa's boy Jack were friends, but Jack doesn't fish much anymore, and so each summer, when the river back home slicks to dust and the grass goes dry-bone brittle, my father packs the cooler with white bread, bologna, and cans of Rainier, and then clamps the topper to the back of the pickup and says to us—my mother, older sister, little brother, and me—"Get in," and we do, and my father hauls ass up into the Beartooth Mountains, where Pa Peters meets us.

And in the half-light of the canyon, Pa Peters is more than worthy of the name grandfather. I am only seven years old, but I can tell already he knows water better than my father, better than any man I have met. He fishes that in-between place—half lake, half river, where the water starts to crash and pull again. His feet are firm in the current, his hands shaking but in each small movement sure. I watch him cast, so long and true and lovely that each swell of line seems to float an hour in the sky, the fine mist of lake water falling, the lure dropping behind a slick rock—and then the strike.

His pole bends, his reel sings, and for a few moments there is this give and take—wild splashing, silver belly flashing—before Pa Peters reaches into the roiling waters and with his trembling hands pulls the cutthroat into the fading mountain light.

He is holding the fish; he is saying something; his lips are moving—but I hear only the roar and fall of river.

COACH DREASE

NOW THEY'RE GIGGLING in the backseat. Most likely Tony's whispered something dirty to Duane—said, "Nuts," or "Knockers," or "Ain't that Nicole Ritterodt a nice piece?"—and Duane has whispered it to Chip, and now Tony, Duane, and Chip are all bugging their eyes out and puffing their cheeks and giggling at Tony's obscene audacity, his priceless comic timing. It helps, of course, that we are just eight years old, and dirty words—though usually misunderstood and misused and mightily rued in the dark hours before sleep—are like gold coins we hoard and pull from our pockets to brighten the dun edges of our already tired boys' days out on the Big Dry.

But I don't care what they're giggling about. Not today.

Today, I'm riding shotgun in Coach's big red dual-cab truck. Today, I'm listening to Coach Drease lecture on baseball, Ford pickups, redheaded women—and how we're going to beat the pants off White Sulphur Springs. And this too, especially this: There is a half rack of Green River pop in the front seat, between Coach and me, and whenever Tony or Chip or Duane wants one, they have to tap me on the shoulder, and I look at Coach, with his left hand draped over the wheel and his right arm stretched across the back of the bench seat, and he works the bulging wad of Copenhagen that is always in his lip and nods. Then, officiously, I hand Tony or Chip or Duane a warm Green River. And Coach—whom I am supposed to call "Sir" or "Mr. Drease" but have been calling "Coach" because I am sure he won't tell my father—has sat me up front here as a kindness, has let me pass out the Green Rivers because these past months my father's muscled chest has begun to cave and sink with cancer. Coach is only eight or ten years out of high school himself, but he knows already he'll work the rest of his days snaking sewer lines and pumping septic tanks, he knows the soft bag of his belly will sag and his shoulders slump before he hits thirty, he knows he'll hope his days away for nothing more than a place to put his feet up and a few beers before the dark comes down. Coach knows what sitting shotgun and a half rack of Green Rivers means. What's more, Coach Drease has only daughters, four of them, and all as small and mincing as their mother, who owns the beauty shop in town. This is his chance, too. Here, he is father to all us Little Leaguers, stepping up to the plate and knocking one over the fence, showing us how it's done. So I am happy, listening to Coach, letting the lemon-lime sweetness of the soda roll down my throat and fizz in my belly, watching the country rise and buckle as we make our way west on Highway 12 and up into the mountains.

"Listen. Listen now," Coach says and slaps the wine-red vinyl of the bench seat, his face going uncharacteristically serious. Chip, Duane, and Tony stop their giggling and lean forward. "We're about to go under a train trestle. I'm going to punch it up to about ninety-five here, boys, because when you go under a train trestle at about ninety-five, you'll hear some things."

"What things?" Tony asks.

"You'll know it when you hear it, bucko. I promise you that. Just keep your ears peeled."

Coach steps hard on the gas. He makes a big show of it, leaning back and putting both hands on the wheel, stiffening his arms. Around the angles of the pickup the wind begins to whistle and keen. Fence posts and cottonwoods whip past, and I lean my head to the window glass. Whatever there is to hear, I want to hear it. I try to block out the wind, the squawky country music on the radio. I listen. I listen.

"Here we go, buckos!" Coach yells, and he scrunches down in his seat like a race-car driver and speeds us under the oily, wooden trestle that spans the river valley—and I hear nothing but wind, a broken lick of steel guitar.

"Hot damn!" Coach says and slaps the steering wheel, a grin—the kind he'd call "shit-eating"—spread across his face. "Did you hear it? Huh?" He takes a big gulp of his Green River and wipes his mouth with the back of his hand. "Damn! That one was a cannon, huh? Like a big old cannon! Sonic boom! Best one I ever heard. Right, Joe?" He winks at me, and I suddenly feel sick. This is too much. The front seat was plenty, and I can't even have pop at home. Yet I know that I must play along, that there is no way out of this. Coach's kindness and my father's tragedy have somehow obligated me. I have a part to play. Coach winks again. "Ain't that right, Joe?"

"Yeah," I say, the untruth soda-sweet and sticky in my throat. "It was loud." But that doesn't feel like enough, so I add, "Damn loud."

Coach slaps me on the shoulder. "Damn loud is right! You boys in back hear it? You heard it, didn't you?" he asks, peering at them in the rearview.

Duane shakes his head and starts to protest, but Tony grabs him and whispers something in his ear. They both laugh. Then Duane whispers to Chip. Chip laughs too. And now they're all laughing and slapping their knees, just like before.

Coach says, "What? You heard it, didn't you? Joe heard it."

"We sure did, *Skinny*," Tony says. "We heard it. Just like Joe said.

Damn loud! Right, buckos?" Duane and Chip fall all over themselves
in fits of laughter.

Coach watches a moment longer, then drops his eyes from the
rearview, looks my way, and shrugs. He takes another drink of Green
River and turns up the radio. The Bronco fills with the crackling
warble of George Jones or Merle Haggard or one of those other sad-
as-can-be-about-the-way-things-turned-out cowboys.

I squirm down into the bench seat, lean against the door and play
with the window crank. I wish he'd left well enough alone. Didn't
you know it was enough, Coach? Skinny? I look at him and in my
mind say it as mean as they did: *Skinny*. I watch him thumb his
hooked nose, then scratch the back of his neck, where his thin, dishwater hair hangs unevenly—and I'm suddenly embarrassed for him,
embarrassed for me, and, as always, mad at my strict, sick father, who
almost never lets me call grownups by their first names, let alone their
nicknames; who even when he was well thought baseball was a waste
of time; who lies now—I can close my eyes to the running river and
the cottonwoods and the far blue mountains, to everything, and see
him—on the old brown couch in the front room of our drafty farmhouse, his bone-burled chest rising with breath. Then falling.

A Fragment from
My Grandfather's Body

A Cheating So-and-So

WHEN I AM nine my father dies, leaving my mother with three hundred acres of farm land along the Musselshell River and three young children. My grandfather is an old man, but he does what he can for us. Tonight, he is teaching my brother and me to play poker. It is April, lambing season, late in the evening, and we're sitting at the kitchen table, killing time as we wait to make the midnight pass through the sheep shed, checking for ewes in labor. My grandfather deals a game of stud—and his face is suddenly stone. My brother, only seven, squeals with delight at a pair of threes, so my grandfather bets him up and clears him out with two jacks.

My mother has long since gone to bed, and my grandfather leans back now, laces his fingers behind his head, and tells us that he nearly shot a man once. It was just after he'd quit school and started cowboying for Frank Schuster out of Broadview, out on the Comanche Flats. One night a bunch of cowboys and hired men were at the poker table, and this fellow was winning hand after hand. My grandfather says, "I saw that cowboy slip an ace from under his arm, and I stood up, drew my gun on him, and called him a cheating so-and-so." He pauses and

51

rubs the gray stubble along his jaw. "My Uncle Okie," he continues, "he stood up beside me and hit me in the face. Knocked me clean out. I woke later that night, Okie telling me not ever to do a damn fool thing like that again."

My grandfather is silent for a long while, so we are silent too, and when he rises and pushes in his chair and tells us it's time, we follow him out into the night. He flicks on the lights of the sheep shed, the low glare and shadow of three widely spaced bare bulbs, and we walk through the herd. We find a ewe down in the dry straw near the back. She is straining hard. We wait and watch, but the lamb's not coming. My grandfather tells us to keep an eye on her. He walks back across the shed to the wash basin and rolls up his sleeves. I glance over and am shocked by the sudden white splash of skin above his wrists. He washes slowly, deliberately, all the way up to his elbows. He doesn't dry his hands, just walks toward us—the drip and steam of water running from his fingers, rising from his arms.

We kneel down beside the ewe. My grandfather tells us to hold her. "Talk to her," he says. So we do. We tell her it will be all right. We look at him as he reaches in and say it again, "It'll be all right." His right hand, then wrist and forearm disappear. His movements are careful, delicate. The ewe lays her head on the straw, closes her eyes to the pain. My grandfather pulls and pulls—and the lamb slips into his hands, hands that nearly took a man's life, and there's blood and afterbirth steaming on the straw, on his arms, everywhere. He runs a finger through the lamb's mouth and sets it near its mother's warmth.

We rise, stiff and suddenly very tired. My grandfather washes up. He turns off the shed lights and walks out into a darkness that is broken only by the faint light of stars.

CLIFTON WILKINS

THE BEARDED MAN in Rapid City wears a dress, and I sleep through Minneapolis. In the backseat a boy with a thin wisp of mustache slips his hand under the green, sequined shirt of a girl laid out across his lap. He reaches her left breast and works it slowly, like dough. When we stop in La Crosse the red-nosed bus driver gives me thirty cents to buy a bag of chips. In the dark, Chicago is cement walls and the smell of burning things, a smear of neon in the rain.

It's nearly Christmas, the first since the funeral, and my life is in this bus—mother, sister, and brother, some stories about a father and a place called North Carolina, the place he once called home. We can't afford to fly or pay for hotels along the way, so we ride the Greyhound, sleep slumped over in our vinyl seats. It takes a smoky week. And we don't even get to eat at restaurants: My mother's packed a paper sack of raisins, tomatoes, and cheese sandwiches, though we run out of raisins and tomatoes halfway through Wisconsin.

The bathrooms at the depots cost a nickel and are always filthy. Sometimes, after someone has to leave, we steal five minutes in one of the plastic seats with little black-and-white TVs. We're traveling clear across the country, but I can't see a thing for all the trees. In glassy freeway light I study road signs, mouth words like "Fancy Gap" and "Roanoke." At night I count each bright stop by marking on my arms. I breathe the smells of sweet wine and smoke, try to memorize the curse words I hear floating up the aisle. If I'm ever bored I beg my sister's deck of cards, her Walkman and Bon Jovi tape, her journal. I punch my brother in the shoulder.

"Stop it now," my mother says. "Just stop it." She's always telling us to go to sleep, to quiet down, to pray a rosary if we're bored. Sometimes, her hands shake against the window glass, her cheeks so slick with tears I can taste the salt. She's so sad, sad and fierce. She holds our tickets out in front of her and shoulders us up to the front of the line. She stands and puts her hands on her hips, tells the young man with the mohawk and the ring in his nose to shut his filthy mouth, she's got children up here, dammit.

The Appalachian Mountains blend into a shaky film of hairpin roads, muddy rivers, wet-black trees marching off into the distance. And, suddenly, we're here.

We shake hands with stoop-backed uncles, their hair Brylcreemed off their foreheads, and get squeezed breathless by sugar-mouthed aunts. We stay a day or two with each pair. One set jams our stockings full of candy and piles wrapped box after wrapped box for us beneath their tree. One aunt takes us to Red Lobster and tells us we can order anything on the menu. One uncle is tall and lean and has a house with big windows and a second-story deck that overlooks a sloping meadow, low mountains in the distance. They all seem so worldly and rich. The one that makes the most sense is my father's oldest brother, Clifton. He's nearly seventy and wears black socks, starched cotton pants, thick-rimmed glasses. His wife, Willie, had a stroke some years ago and half her face hangs at a kind of angle. Though the factory down the street shakes the foundation, their house is plain and neat. Willie cooks biscuits and serves them with molasses every morning. They don't make a fuss or play with us, like all the others. Uncle Clifton sits at the table and drinks his coffee, turns and snaps the morning paper. My mother tells us after the war he started work at the textile factory, where he spent the next forty years, and used his wages to help my grandparents stay on the farm and raise my father.

Near the end of our visit, all the aunts and uncles—save Uncle Clifton and Aunt Willie—drive us out into the country. They walk us down old, overgrown farm roads, tall grass and trees and vines, piles of dun leaves to crunch and scatter. I find it hard to believe my father ever lived in this wet, ripe place. We pull open the rot-wood door of the tobacco shed, breathe the ancient spice and musk. And then, when we get to the old house, they all just stand there, telling stories, so my brother and I take off running circles around the ruin.

I run and run and run the questions in my blood: Can this really be the house where some frowning woman they call my grandmother birthed ten children and raised the seven that lived? Where some grim man they call my grandfather tried year after year to grow a little cotton, cure a little tobacco, and pay down the credit at the bank? How could a farm fail here, where the rain always falls? Could we trade rain for acres? Could we bargain grass for grass? Why do some have this and others have that? Can the muddy, round-cheeked boy they talk about really be the hard plainsman who was my father?

And why does my mother touch everything as if in her hands it might shatter?

DONNIE LAIRD

FIRST THING IN the morning, fat Donnie Laird turns his welding
rig onto our road and comes raising a rooster tail of dust fast down
the gravel and bangs on the screen door with his ham of a fist and
announces to my mother that he'll go ahead and fix the boys' basketball hoop.

I didn't know anyone had told him about our hoop: how the other
day I'd wanted to lower it so my brother and I could dunk, so to reach
the screws to slip the hoop down the pole I took the pickup keys without permission and with the tailgate down backed over the cement
pad and up to the pole. I hung my hand over the wheel and angled
the mirrors, like I'd seen done, and told my brother to direct me—
but neither of us knew what we were doing. I slammed the wedge
of the tailgate right into the pole, and it buckled and cracked, began
to bend, which meant the new basketball hoop and level cement pad
we'd begged and begged our mother for—told her it meant so much
to us because Tony and everyone else had one, and without a hoop
and pad to practice on we wouldn't be any good when we got to junior high and would then be made merciless fun of, so please, please

we absolutely have to have a new hoop and cement pad—was just-like-that useless.

And maybe no one had told Donnie. Maybe he came raising a rooster tail of dust down the gravel just to see if there was anything he could do, because that's what my father's old friends are always doing: stopping by sad-eyed and grim-mouthed, their feed-store ball caps twisted up in their hands, staring at their boots and asking if there's anything, anything at all, they can do. Most of the time my mother thanks them and sends them away. Though they are strong, they cannot haul my father up and out of this dry ground. Though they are skilled farmers and ranchers, a day on the tractor or a night in the lambing shed won't mean much in the long run. They too loved my father, and like us they are bewildered and brokenhearted. Though they ask if there's anything they can do, they ask not for us but for themselves—they ask out of the selfishness of grief.

Which is fine. Which is probably as it should be.

Donnie probably stepped out of his rig that morning and saw the bent hoop and knew right then and there what he could do. He might have even thought for a moment, before he put his fist to the screen door, about the boy who did it and what it would mean to have such a mistake erased. For standing here in our doorway with his stink of liquor and tobacco spit and ammonia, I imagine shame and expiation are much on Donnie's mind.

My mother nods, accepting this kindness, and then lets the screen door slap closed. My brother and I are excited. We pull on tennis shoes and deer-hide gloves and go out to help. While Donnie readies the welder, we haul out his tools. I grab a big rusty box and small rusty box, my brother totes over a five-gallon bucket and fills it with well water. Donnie lights a cigarette and rubs at his eyes, tells me the other welding helmets are in the cab, behind the seat. I crank open the truck door and see a pillow of greasy clothes on the bench seat, a cardboard suitcase and a bottle of whiskey on the floor. I push the seat forward and grab the masks and consider that Donnie has probably not been home for days, has not seen his wife and daughters—who go to our church and live up the road from us in a double-wide trailer near the river—in a long, long time.

While he readies the welder, Donnie has my brother and I take wire brushes to the scarred metal around the bend. Beyond my grandfather, I don't often see men up close anymore, so while we scrape at the flaking paint I sneak looks over at Donnie. He's quite tall, must be up over six feet, and though his face is round and wide, his eyes and nose and mouth are close together, pinched in. His skin, like the skin of most everyone around here, is umber from the sun, and when he takes off his cap to wipe the sweat from his face with his shirt sleeve, there is a stark, pink-white line across his forehead. My grandfather is always telling me, stepping back and putting up his fists, that he's right at fighting weight: 180 pounds. Donnie seems twice the size of my grandfather. He is thick as shelves across the chest, his arms and legs muscled and enormous. Donnie is almost too big. I don't exactly like the look of him. And he wears a button-up work shirt, dark blue, the very kind my father wears in the picture on the piano, which makes me wonder if this is just what you do when you are a man: get big and thick and wear a blue shirt to work.

Once Donnie has the welder in order, and we have the puckered metal scraped and brushed, we all three of us put our shoulders to the pole and bend it straight. Donnie gulps at the air, like some huge fish, his untucked shirt waving over the hairy, pearled curve of his stomach. He wipes his sweating forehead on his sleeve and motions to the masks, and I hand him one, and my brother and I screw the others onto our heads and flip the visors down. The day goes dark—until Donnie sparks the torch.

He lays, like I thought he would, a thick bead directly in the metal scar, but then, opposite that, where the pole looks more or less straight and fine, he welds a long rectangle of tempered steel, the width of it sticking six inches straight back.

I think a fin, a wing, maybe Donnie's signature or bit of artifice—but I am so happy to have the evidence of my wrongdoing made right that I don't ask any questions, don't discover that this steel wing is a kind of truss and carries the whole weight of the hoop, keeps it from slowly folding over on itself again.

Though I know some few things, I don't understand all the forces at work here, the mechanics of tension, moment, and node. How twice the strength is needed to come straight at something. How what is still is charged and what is hastened is dead. How bread becomes flesh, how flesh becomes dust, how the heart is bread and flesh and dust—the way with a rag Donnie slops well water to cool the weld and picks up his clanking tools, and my brother and I thank him and shake his heavy, trembling hand, and though he will in a few years abandon his wife and daughters and dedicate himself to liquor and other oblivions, we think of him kindly and often.

EDITH FREEMAN

IN MY AUNT Edith's studio I am quiet. I have not been told to be quiet, I am just quiet, for her studio—with its intricate tools and brushes and long-necked lamps on benches, its smells of paint and standing water and shaved pine—seems to me a place to be quiet, watchful, even reverent.

I shut the door, slowly, and stand off to the side. I lean up against the wall with my hands behind me, at the small of my back. I feel with my palms and fingertips the whorled, rough-cut boards, and I watch my Aunt Edith, who is really my great aunt, my grandfather's older sister. Her back is to me, one lock of silvery hair hanging down about her face. With her full, calloused hands, hands nearly as big as a man's, she pulls the wet print from the face of the wood—all orange and fish-belly and washed blue; maybe, I think, the scab hills south of Billings at daybreak—and she studies and studies it, the colors and densities and textures, and finally hangs it up with the others to dry.

Aunt Edith makes prints. She lays a grainy, rough-cut slab of hardwood before her and takes up knife, plane, chisel, gouge, and adze, and she peels away strips and curlicues of red-yellow wood, and slowly, slowly, the picture-scape takes shape. Here is one of an old homesteader's

shack, just like the log cabin in back of our house, with the far corner settling, seeming to melt back into the earth. Here are the thousand knuck-
lings of a sagebrush. Here the scabrous and delicate trunks of jack pines.
The carvings themselves are lovely, but when she drips and swirls the
paint onto them and presses a sheet of paper against them—then, something astonishing happens: The world thins to paper, to shape and color.
Aunt Edith's prints are of the world but above the world. They seem to
me like the best of stories: They wake me up, make me look again and
again, my breath fairly running from my lips.

Aunt Edith turns back to the paint-wet wood before her and considers. Her hands at her hips, she studies the grain, the colors—and I
wait and wait. Like her younger brother, my grandfather, Aunt Edith
is sure and economical in each movement of herself; if she were to pick
up the gouge, a watery runnel of wood would open for her. Yet they
are different too. Though my grandfather may take a quick moment
to see how best to go at a thing, once he decides, he decides, and works
then steadily, inexorably—chunking shovelful after shovelful of furnace coal into the cellar until the metal shovel grates and screams
against the metal pickup bed—to the end. Not Aunt Edith. She thinks
and ponders. She turns her head one way, and then the other way, and
I see the corner of her wide mouth turn up into a smile. Still, she does
nothing. She looks, she thinks, she smiles. I have heard others make
fun of Aunt Edith for her languid ways, but I see something here not
unlike the cold quiet of a church or the charged look of a penitent at
prayer, and maybe this is why I am quiet here: Her thoughtfulness and
care says there is something happening here beyond work or play; her
reverence says that here is another world that needs attending, too.

"Oh," Aunt Edith says, turning now, her wrinkled face sliding into
a wider smile. "I didn't hear you come in. Goodness, how quiet you
were! Shall we get some ice cream? Hmm? I think maybe I would
like a bowl of ice cream. What about you, Joe?"

I am too old to be talked to this way, fussed over and pampered, but Aunt Edith never had children of her own and doesn't know, and so I don't mind. Also, I very much want a bowl of vanilla ice cream dotted with raspberries fresh from her garden. "Yes," I say. "I think I would like a bowl of ice cream, too."

Later, we go to dinner. I get ready in the third-floor bathroom. Aunt Edith's house is grand and yellow and sits on the rimrocks above the Yellowstone River and the city of Billings. You can see forever out this window, clear to the Big Horn and Beartooth Mountains. You can see as well the streets and traffic and tall hotels and shiny bank buildings of downtown Billings, which is where we're going for dinner. I know I must clean up and dress nicely. I scrub my face with soap, comb my hair. I tuck my shirt into my jeans and lace up my best sneakers. I rush down the first flight of stairs, which curves around and down the cone-topped turret of the house, and step more carefully down the next flight of stairs, in case Aunt Edith is ready and waiting for me. She isn't. I sit at the dark dining room table, flip through her piles of journals, which are smaller than magazines and have tiny type and long articles. I study, in the photo above the table, the lean, bearded face of Aunt Edith's dead husband. He looks kind enough, I guess. Maybe a little disappointed. He failed, I have heard, at farming, and Aunt Edith supported them by teaching school. After he died, Aunt Edith started painting and making prints instead. Her work hangs in all those bank buildings downtown now, is up at the Yellowstone Art Museum, too. I even see her prints in the color inset pages of these journals I flip through. Some cousin told me she sells each print for a thousand dollars. Aunt Edith is an artist. It's thrilling and obscene even to say it, to say *artist*, which sounds like the look of wine or pictures of Spain. Aunt Edith is as well an atheist, which is not thrilling but troublesome. I don't quite understand what all being an atheist entails, but I think it means her dead husband will not be waiting for her in heaven, like my mother says my father will be waiting for me. I think it means as well that Aunt Edith will not go to heaven at all.

Yet Aunt Edith doesn't seem worried, smiling and stepping from her room now in dark slacks and a long-sleeved, silky blouse, silver at her neck and on her fingers, her silver hair pulled back in a tight bun.

"I've been waiting for you."

"Thank you," she says. "Thank you for waiting." In her finery she looks like my Aunt Edith and not like my Aunt Edith. "Shall we have some dinner?"

"Yes," I say.

Dinner is at a Chinese restaurant downtown. The doorways arc above our heads, and there is the sound of stone and water. A low light on the faces of couples leaning toward one another. The hostess bows to us, her long hair midnight dark, and takes us to a table. This is the first time I have ever eaten at a Chinese restaurant, the first time I have ever eaten anywhere where there are reservations and small menus without prices and waitresses who don't write anything down but nod knowingly. In fact, I could probably count on one hand the times I have eaten at a sit-down restaurant. We don't even get to stop at McDonald's most of the time when we are in Billings, my mother always packing cheese sandwiches for lunch instead.

Aunt Edith knows the names of things and orders now for both of us. While we wait we talk about the prints she was working on today, about books, about the news, about what things I like to study in school. The waitress comes with steaming tea and some kind of sour soup, plates of rice and orange-colored chicken thighs and thinly sliced beef with red peppers. It's all new and strange and beautiful. Before we eat, I say, "Wait!" I look up at my Aunt Edith. "What are the names? I want to know the names of everything."

A Fragment from
My Grandfather's Body

A HARD RUN ACROSS THE FLATS

WE WALK DOWN the fence line, hot wind in our lungs and the hot sun in the sky. We have left the pickup at the corner of the pasture, carried our hammers and fencing pliers and staples in steel buckets, and walked the fence today. The hardpan gumbo cracks beneath our boots; dust has worked deep into our deer-hide gloves and the seams of our blue jeans.

I ask my grandfather for the story about his horse, Nine Spot. He looks down the long miles of fence, over swells of bunchgrass and a dry creek, and we sit, our backs against an old railroad tie corner post. He unknots the red silk handkerchief at his throat and wets it with canteen water and tips up his cowboy hat and wipes his face, then hands the handkerchief to me. He pulls cheese sandwiches and plums wrapped in thick brown paper, still cold, from one of the steel buckets. We unwrap our sandwiches and bite into our plums, and he tells me Nine Spot was an ornery little mare, blue-black and fast. He tells me he was working for his uncle, riding for strays out on the Comanche Flats, where the world is one part grass and two parts sky—and suddenly it's 1931, and my grandfather is sixteen and thin as a willow whip in the saddle. Some months ago he quit school to cowboy for a living, and he lets Nine Spot go now at a gallop, not for any reason other than they both love a hard run across the flats.

And I know this story already, know something spooks Nine Spot—sometimes it's a rattler, other times a wrong step near a gopher hole—but the boy who is my grandfather always falls from the saddle, his foot twisted in the stirrup, and Nine Spot is white-eyed and scared, still running, and the prairie rips and twists and burns beneath my grandfather—he's lost his hat, feels his shirt tear and slip over his shoulders, his leg stretch and snap, and Nine Spot turns and finally bucks him free and keeps running, and my young grandfather skids to a stop in the desolate heart of the flats, broken and utterly alone, the dust settling around him and on him.

And this is the part I want to hear, so I lean into his breath as he grabs hold of a sagebrush, pulls himself up to it, grabs another, pulls, then another, and over a mile later he collapses in the gravel of Pretty Prairie Road, where Ollie Johnson, the Maytag repairman out of Billings, finds him. My grandfather wakes as Ollie hauls him into his Model T. His jeans are torn, and he can see the bright bone spurred through the meat of his thigh. My young grandfather reaches down to touch the torn end of his own femur—and ends his story.

My heart's racing, half my sandwich forgotten in my lap. My grandfather sucks the stone of his plum a moment and then pitches it off into the sagebrush. He re-knots his handkerchief and gets up, an old man again, and walks down the fence line. I see the hitch in his step, one leg an inch or two shorter than the other ever since the doctor set the bone wrong, and now he leans on a wood post, turns to me, and adds something that I have never heard before: "It hurt like hell, pulling myself across the prairie like that. It would've been awful easy just to lay myself down and look at the sun."

This comes like a cold north wind that bends and breaks the grass, freezes the horse trough hard. My world, battered as it is, does not have to be this way. It doesn't have to be at all. He wasn't thinking of me but must have been thinking of me all those years ago out on the prairie, pulling his ragged legs through the cactus and dry grass.

I stare at my child's hands. If he dies out there on the Comanche Flats all those years ago, I die too. His bent body—sun dark, seventy-odd years of wind and dust—is somehow my body.

FRANK HOLLOWELL

WHEN THE OTHER elementary school teachers aren't looking, Mr. Hollowell lets us play tackle football back of the school. He even plays tackle football with us, three or four of us hanging off him, our thin arms wrapped around his neck, his waist, thighs like the trunks of pines. He is short and stocky, his black hair bright in the slanting, early-recess sunlight, and he looks—oddly, uncannily, even my mother says so—like a younger, healthier version of my father. I tell him this once while we are back in the huddle getting ready for the next play. And he looks at me and smiles and says, "Well, okay, but you better block for me now, because I'm going to take this one in for a touchdown." So when he calls "Hike!" I do: I block one boy, two boys—and, sure enough, touchdown.

When we go back inside, he reads out loud to us from *Where the Red Fern Grows* or *The Outsiders*. He sits on a stool and plays old Hank Williams tunes on his guitar, lets us get up and sing and dance around. He jokes and kids and slaps us wonderfully hard on the back. Then, when someone has a birthday—say, Wendell Williamson or Ruthie Aasgaard, or some other kid whose parents everyone knows won't bring in cupcakes—Mrs. Hollowell comes to our class with all kinds of treats. She is slender and blond, and I think she is the most beautiful woman I have ever seen. So does Mr. Hollowell. He holds her hand in front of us, teases her, calls her "honey" and "darling." They have a new baby girl who sleeps and coos and is as beautiful as the both of them. They are just out of college, and they aren't like so many out here on the Big Dry. They have ambitions beyond a good footstool and a six-pack of Coors. They do things; they go places. They are full of what this town lacks: possibility. And as if they were cupcake frosting or Green River pop, none of us can get enough of them.

So when my father finally dies, I am sad for a while, but then I am happy because Mr. Hollowell brings his guitar to my father's funeral and sings, and when he hits that last note, he starts crying. Everyone's crying, and I'm crying, and I'm so happy. And when I finally come back to school and walk in the classroom door, Mr. Hollowell starts crying again. He lets me skip math, lets me stay after and finish my homework with him, buys me a Snickers and a Mountain Dew. I don't understand it. I don't care. Soon, I'm staying after every day. Soon, he is driving me home, telling my mother it's no problem, even firing up the tractor, doing the spring planting my father had planned during his sickness. Soon, Mr. Hollowell is showing me how to irrigate, taking me out on my father's motorbike, telling me to step into the ditch and let the dirty water curl around my rubber hip boots, saying, "Don't worry. You'll stay dry." Saying, "Tamp those dams down tight. We've got to flood these fields good to bring green grass up on this dry land."

I'm delirious with his attention. I take seed. I sway and rise.

I am suddenly picked early—or at least in the first half—for football and basketball, chased around at recess by Nicole Ritterodt, who even starts telling people I'm her boyfriend. Mr. Hollowell gives me extra work when I finish mine before everyone else. He gets me moved up a grade for reading and math, somehow finagles a way for me to write the elementary-school editorial each month in the junior-high newspaper. And here, suddenly, I find myself without peer. If you want to win at kickball at recess, you need Tony or Chip on your team, but no one can do fractions as fast as I can. No one knows as many answers in the quiz bowl. And Mr. Hollowell slaps a sticker on my paper and hands me another book.

Then, on my tenth birthday, Mr. Hollowell takes me to his folks' place along the Yellowstone River. There, in that always-wet valley, we walk in the pine woods and fish for catfish all afternoon. His brother, a football star, practices spirals with me. His square-jawed father lets me take the four-wheeler out for a drive. Late in the night I sit with Mrs. Hollowell by the fire and sip hot cocoa as Mr. Hollowell and his brother and his father pass around a bottle of whiskey. His father strikes a chord on the mandolin, his brother lets loose a jangling rhythm on the banjo, and Mr. Hollowell strums the guitar, begins to sing.

And so, when Mr. Hollowell moves away at the end of the year, I will more than need someone to take his place, someone—no, some man—to throw me the football and hand me a book, to fill the space made gaping not by my father's death but by Mr. Hollowell's merciful and immoderate attention.

I will look, I still look, I am looking for a father.

III.

I was told to worship

the first book I read,

the book of waters,

written in a dry year.

—PHILIP LEVINE

Burn Barrel

SOMETIMES, AFTER DINNER, my mother would ask me to take out the trash and burn it. During the day, I didn't mind this chore, hoped in fact that it would be given to me and not to my brother, for if you didn't dump the trash, you had to dump the chicken pail, an old ice cream bucket of moldy slices of cheese and melon rinds and coffee grounds and whatever other kitchen scraps a chicken might peck at. The trouble with the chicken pail was you had to face the bandy-legged rooster, always strutting and working his long neck back and forth and clacking and snapping his beak, and maybe even the squawking geese or the black-faced buck sheep, chewing their cuds and bumping heads with a loud crack. Most of the time, dumping the garbage was the less fearful chore.

Except at night. If my father was not working late in the garage or the sheep shed—which he didn't much, once he was sick—there was no light on the plains save the moon and the small holes of stars. On a cloudy night, then, or during a new moon, the sky went liquid black, flooding everything—the known road and corrals and trees off along the river—in a lake bottom of blackness. Except for the dim porch light, nothing sounded that dark for miles. It flowed over and around you, surrounding your each and every step, lapping at your thin arms and small hands and paper sack of garbage, fist of wooden matches. And each step only deepened the blackness, made you aware of new pools and riffles of night.

I was a fearful boy: My heart like some small, impassioned animal slamming at the bone cage of my chest, I'd toss the garbage sack in the burn barrel and pull the matches across the iron two at time—blue spark and fast orange flare—and toss them in one after the other and breathe as the darkness rolled back, slipped like water off the body of the rising fire.

This was how I managed it, with fire. I seldom entered my fear but found ways to beat it back. When my cancer-wracked father yelled at me, yelled and swore at me because I was a boy and had done something wrong or was in his way somehow, yelled at me because there was in him a turning pain that bit down into his bones, I ran to the shelterbelt. I ran and squatted in the tall grass and clenched in my little fists the weeds and grass, to anchor me there, safe and away. I stayed hidden, in the tall grass, away from him.

To this day, I remember so little of my father. I can see the wall of his back as I burrowed into my parents' bed as a small boy. I remember him raising his rifle and taking a step toward a yearling sheep ready for butchering. I remember his tamed magpie, Maggie, dropping out of the sky and onto his shoulder, the way he loved and teased the bird, his shirt pocket full of the cat food Maggie craved. I remember as well flashes of a day in Billings—maybe he was hauling a pickup load of culled ewes to the auction yards, maybe he had to get a part for the swather at Tractor Supply—but no matter the reason he brought me with him. It was just the two of us. I sat on the pickup's bench seat and like him studied the road, hooked my arm out my open window. He bought me a hamburger at a café in the heights and somewhere a helium balloon. On the way home, in a grocery store parking lot, I think, I accidently let the balloon go, and my father, in his creased jeans and going-to-town shirt, with its red checks and shiny snaps, came to me and comforted me, told me my balloon would float and float and float down to some other little boy, who would become my friend. I remember even the gray-blue sky, the balloon slipping up and into it.

I know he took us fishing, and I remember Pa Peters and the great slopes of scree high on the mountains and the crashing river water and six-packs of beer and strawberry pop cooling in the mossy creek, but I don't remember my father. I have been told my brother and I often followed our father around as he worked in the garage or in the shed, and I remember the warm stink of sheep and straw and shit, trays of greasy tools and the quick knocking of the air compressor, but I don't remember him. I know he often had friends over to drink beer and laugh with, that each fall his college buddies came out to our place to hunt antelope, and I do remember them, their beards and silver cans and cigarettes, but I do not remember him.

I remember only a few fading moments of my father. And then I remember him angry, then I remember him dead. That is what I remember. I think maybe this is how I managed my fear and then my grief, which was just another kind of fear: by tossing a match on every memory of my father that might burn.

FLOOD

IF THERE HAD been a flood, a true flood, the dark and frothing waters sluing across the plains, our house would most certainly have sheared from its moorings, drifted like a drunk, and sunk.

The foundation was bad, a great long crack in the stone and cement of the south wall of the basement. When a summer storm thundered through, or when a chinook wind came whistling up from the south and the snow melted in a matter of hours, water sieved through the dry ground and poured from that crack. The plaster came away in chunks then, and the water came even quicker, muddier. My brother and I swept the water to the sump pump in the corner, shoveled out the mud. More than once, the pump burned out trying to keep pace with the rain. Then, until we could get to town to get the right part, the whole basement would fill and stink and mosquitoes would begin to breed.

Beyond the sodden books and ruined rug and shorted freezer, those hundreds of pounds of spoiled meat, we knew the house itself might not hold. The south foundation wall might buckle and collapse and then the house above lean and fall. One summer I dug a trench around the perimeter of the house, some three feet down, and dumped in bag after bag of powdered bentonite, which hardens when water hits it, and then I packed dirt back over the bentonite, which is as well a terrible carcinogen. We were hoping the bentonite would waterproof the foundation, but with every afternoon storm, water still seeped and ran into the basement. My mother had a contractor come in and pour a wide sidewalk around the foundation. That didn't help either, and the contractor told us the only thing left to do was lift the house up into the air and tear out the foundation and redo it. We didn't have the money for that. We shut the basement door. Let it flood, hoped the wall would hold.

The foundation, though, was just one thing among many. We had mice in all the closets, ants in the sugar drawer, mealworms wriggling in the flour, millers and moths hatching eggs in the ceiling. In the summer our little air conditioner cooled maybe a room and a half. In the winter we rubbed our stinging eyes and coughed as coal smoke rose through the vents. The kitchen counters were knife-scarred and stained of meat and other things, the wallpaper in the bathroom peeled off in sheets.

Yet through it all our old house, cobbled together from the ruins of homesteader's shacks, weathered and stood. The waters never rose high enough, I guess, and the stone, even broken, was stronger than it looked.

Mountain

FOR THREE DAYS it has rained.

The little creek we're camped on rushes straight down the valley, ditch-fast and muddy. The limbs we drag back to camp are so green with sap or rotten with rainwater they will not burn. We cannot light a fire. We have caught no trout. We huddle at the table, musty blankets draped over our shoulders.

We are here, a hundred miles from home and holed up in our tiny camper, because my father is dead. Or rather, we are here because when my father was alive he took us to the Beartooth Mountains every summer. During some scorched July week, my father would park his tractor and pack the old forest green Coleman cooler and drive us up to Mystic Lake, where we'd fish for cutthroat and hike switchback trails and breathe the cedar-clean air. Those good days the mountains were like the many stone hands of God, the sun always bright and the air crisp and just cool. Pa Peters would most often meet us there, and he'd tell us where the fish were biting. I'd wade up to my knees and cast and cast and finally haul in a rainbow. My brother and I might explore the far side of the lake, where we saw a mother black bear and two cubs once, or my sister might hike up the canyon with us to the waterfall. Come evening, we sat on stumps and hunks of granite and stuck marshmallows on long willow sticks. My sister toasted them lightly over the coals, and I blackened them in the flames, and my brother sat far back from the fire and ate them raw, and my mother and father sipped beer and laughed and told stories—the wavery dome of firelight illuminating all that mattered in the world.

We are here because my uncles are too busy and my grandfather too old, because my friends' fathers fish only too-warm reservoirs for bass and catfish. We are here because my mother grieves hard as iron for my father, for her fatherless children, and so she has by herself hitched the secondhand camper-trailer to the pickup and packed the tackle box and the cooler and hauled us west across Montana to the smaller but closer Castle Mountains—where each day the rain has come at us hard and slantways. Where each day we fish the creek and fail, try a fire and fail. Where we huddle now in the camper, play another hand of cards, which my sister wins like always. Where dinner is again cold canned chili topped with cheese and onions.

We are out of bounds now, the known world spinning from beneath us, the story told so far and forgotten, no God but gray sky, gone trout, and a sputtering camper heater. We eat our chili cold. We fold the table down into a bed. And in the mountain cold, the four of us fall asleep.

Yet what a time it was. Like a slanting rain, I want to whisper across the years: It was enough. There was a mountain. Fir and cedar leaned in around us. Even for the rain I had a can of strawberry soda cooling in the creek. One day we put on ponchos anyway and hiked to Elk Mountain. In the forest proper the rain came sparingly, and later the sun shone a moment on the meadow. We picked tiny purple flowers, and put our lips to the rock's lips and drank from the spring.

We lay back in the wet grass and told stories to one another and didn't worry if they were true. Astonishing, really, that we made it there at all, that in the years to come we would make it back most every summer. Mother, I don't know how you did what you did. It would have been easy to say enough. To say I'm tired. To say I tried, to throw your hands up in the air. Most everyone expected it, I imagine. Expected you to let whatever rain came soak us and whatever wind blow us like dry weeds across creation.

But here you are, carrying a fire in your hands.

You'd gone down the road, in the rain, and found someone who'd been camped there for weeks and had a load of good, dry kindling. You must have begged an armful—what force and fury, I think now, to knock on a stranger's door and beg an armful—for when we peek out you have the fire burning, even for the rushing rain, and the wet branches we'd gathered steaming dry on the rocks around the pit. That fire burns hot and high, it burns all night. And the creek in the next valley, we discover, runs deeper, colder. In the morning we go out with jigs and hoppers and corn and catch a mess of brookies. My sister loads them on the stringer, and then like dirty heroes we march back to camp. Squatting by the creek, you show us how to gut them, rock a whetted jackknife from anus up to jaw and then with a quick rip pull the gills and guts from the meat.

As if you knew our luck would turn, you have the fire already burnt to coals, bacon grease slicking an iron skillet. You dust the fish with salt and flour and fry them whole. The pink flesh falls hotly off the bones. We eat it. And are filled.

THE BOOK OF WATER

For a quick moment my father held my red, wet body. Then he set me in my mother's arms and drove through the star-cut spring dark the ninety miles north and east to our dryland sheep and hay farm. There, he pulled on his hip boots, grabbed a shovel, and trudged north to open the irrigation headgate, to bring the surfeit of a season's snowmelt to our fields. And that summer there was not just a second, or even a rare third, but a mythical fourth cutting of hay.

When the traveling priest came, they baptized me in a barrel of runoff rainwater. The dirt road muddy and rutted, the air heavy with the stink of puddles and bright hollyhocks, the priest took me from my father and plunged me down and down. Water pouring like sudden rivers from each thick sleeve of his vestments, he lifted me from rain to sky.

THE SKY IS white and wide, and I walk the dusty mile down Queens Point Road to what's left of the Musselshell River. At the old one-lane iron bridge I slip between fence wires and clamber down the crumbling bank, the earth hot on my hands, the dry weeds and clumps of grass I hang onto cracking off at the burnt roots.

It is the summer of thirst and fire: the snowpack already gone in the mountains, the coulees and seasonal creeks bone dry, two hundred miles away Yellowstone aflame. And the grasshoppers, a true plague of them, deviling the fields and taking the range right down to pear cactus and dust. I clap my hands together now over the swaying seed heads of a stand of tall river-fed grass and crush a dozen grasshoppers with this single blow. I have set myself these tasks: Each day I must say my rosary for rain and kill a hundred hoppers. I clap and clap and, when I feel I've met my mark, wipe my grimy hands on my jeans. I kick off my shoes then and wade out into one of the few stagnant pools of water that still spot the stone belly of the river. For most of the year the Musselshell is the only running water that cuts the hundreds of prairie miles between the Missouri and the Yellowstone. But it's midsummer now. And the Musselshell too has dried. I gather a pile of smooth, palm-sized rocks. I weigh them in my hands, spit on them, rub dust from their faces. In one of the pools a few carp dart about, their fins and tails breaking the shallow water here and there. I take aim.

With a barrage of six or eight well-thrown stones, I drive a fat one onto the gravel. I come closer. The fish flaps and twists and sucks at the air, its bright scales paling with dust.

I SUCK at the jug a moment more and set it heavily on the counter. It is deep summer, and I've just opened our second-to-last jug of drinking water, which means we will soon take a trip to Lewiston.

We can't drink our well water. We can't even feed it to our houseplants—a hard, white crust will form along the pots and the stems will yellow and bend. Nearly all the wells in this high plains country bring up water that's slow, stinking, and alkaline; water that tastes of thistles and rotten eggs; water that'll hollow you out quick if you drink it. They used to haul train cars of drinking water to all these Milwaukee Road stops, a big rusty tank parked near the tracks, but now we have to scavenge our own—every mudroom and basement and outbuilding full of old milk jugs and big five-gallon totes. Most people drive to Forsyth or Billings, where the water's drinkable and ordinary, but we're lucky: We have relatives in Lewiston, where the water comes straight off the mountain.

We drive the hundred and fifty miles north and west on a Sunday, go to mass with my mother's brother and his family at their big church with real stained glass, and then, after the adults go inside to have coffee and tea, our cousins help us fill jugs. My sister twists on the spigot and takes the hose and fills the jugs, and my brother tightens the caps behind her. The rest of us haul the full, capped jugs to the pickup. The afternoon light is cool and lemony, the jugs slick and cold in our hands. Soon, we are happily wet, splashing and spraying one another, shouting and laughing in the water-jeweled front lawn.

When we're done, and everyone is inside or wrapped in towels on the front porch, I turn the spigot on once more and drink for a moment from the hose. What a thing, I think, rare as a roller coaster or a sit-down dinner at a restaurant: to drink right from the hose.

I drink for a long time. I breathe in the mountain light, wipe at my cold lips with the back of my hand. Then drink again.

I WAKE in the dark to the beeping of my alarm clock. In its low, green light I climb down from my bunk, stand and watch for a moment the rise and fall of my younger brother's chest, then pull on jeans and a T-shirt and make my way down the hallway. I step quietly past my mother's closed door. She is alone in there, tired and alone, and I step quietly past her door and turn through the kitchen, moon glow on the linoleum, and step down into the porch, where I fumble for my hip boots, pull a hat over my head. Leaning just outside the screen door, I find our one good long-handled shovel. And then, I am ready.

I begin at the ditch, where the water still pours from the cutouts I gouged in the bank yesterday afternoon, and walk down the field, along the raised dike, until I come to the lip of the irrigation water, maybe forty feet from the back fence. I must wait until the water has flooded the entire dike, so I sit and chew an alfalfa stem and wait. Beneath me the soil cracks and settles, though to call it soil is not exactly correct. There is no topsoil to speak of: only dirt, pale and dry, alkaline swirls twisting through the hard crust of it. The water, on its way to the back fence, burbles and seeps into fissures and clefts, spreads slowly around the roots of grass and alfalfa. But even for this irrigated flood, the land is dry right down to bedrock: I close my eyes and in the darkness behind my lids see the sun rise, the fields steam, and water snakes twist beneath rocks. I see everything go down to dust.

I open my eyes. Spit the alfalfa's green pith on the ground and stand and shake thoughts of sun and dust and snakes from my head. The water has reached the fence. I walk back down the dike, toward the ditch, the mud of the field sucking at my hip boots. At the ditch bank, before wading in to plug the cutouts and pull the canvas dam, letting the water rush and roll down the ditch to the next dam, where I'll dig new cutouts and flood the next two dikes, I pause.

The still, brimming ditch perfectly reflects the sky: little milk spots of stars poured in the watery dark. Carefully, I step into the moon.

I HOIST a fifty-pound bag of dry cement on my knee and pour it from the lip of the rectangular hole that will soon be the Melstone Public Swimming Pool.

Though the noon sun is nearly unbearable, everyone is smiling and joking, because we are building a pool. Melstone, the little outpost town my family calls home, sits at the north bend of the Musselshell River, the Big Dry opening up to the east. Around a hundred people live in the city limits. Another fifty or sixty farm and ranch in the scrubland about. So when the cement is solid and the diving boards are bolted down, Melstone, Montana, will be the smallest incorporated town in the United States with a public swimming pool. Now, Melstone isn't the kind of place where taxes and public projects are looked on kindly, but we're so dry no one cares right now about ideology—farm wives have brought heaping plates of cookies and cold jugs of lemonade, the volunteer fire department has driven over a truck to hose us down every hour or so, and we all wear neon T-shirts featuring a cartoon cowboy trying to cool off in a horse trough. *Boy,* the cramped ranch hand laments, *we sure could use a pool in Melstone!*

I don't really like the T-shirts. Bright green, a grinning horse standing on his hind hooves—they seem to me undignified, childish, like we are somehow delighted by our forsaken circumstances: less than twelve inches of rain a year, creeks that slick to mud come May, wells pumping water so alkaline you shouldn't even slop it into your dog's dish. T-shirts or not, though, we'll have this one wet place, I think, as I smooth the cement with a scoop shovel, as the sun bears down, the plains wind splashing dust over all our faces.

I STEP and splash through the swampy water and am still dry in my good rubber hip boots. I think that there is nothing like this: the weight and heft of water against dry skin. It pleases me, as does this unexpected flood in the valley, the first I've ever seen: every slough and bend running like a river, the fields new lakes, catfish gathering in the deep channels of the ditches.

Though I know these few days of flood will probably do as much damage as the last three summers of drought—the alfalfa will rot and drown, and the hay, when it comes, will be thin and full of weeds—right now I don't care. We're always in the middle of a drought, and this flood is some kind of miracle. I have never seen such water.

I come to a rise of land and step up onto it. I feel reckless, full of the wing beats of birds. I look at my boots and wiggle my dry, invisible toes. I smile. My toes are thirsty birds, I think, as I sit in the dirt and pull off my boots, run barefooted back into the flood.

BLACKBIRDS SETTLE in my wake, begin working the sour ground I've just raked the cut hay off of.

I swallow the dust and chaff in my throat, glance forward, turning the black wheel ever so slightly to keep the tractor curving with the curve of the field. One hand still on the tractor's black wheel, the other gripping the back of the iron seat, I look behind me and see the black-birds and the backward wedge of the hay rake, circled forks snapping at the dirt, funneling the cut prairie grass and clover into a single windrow that winds the field thick enough for the baler to jaw up.

Forward and back, forward and back—always careful to keep the tractor from slipping and skittering down the side of the hill, the windrow continuous and thick—this is what I do. Since we leased our place near the river, I no longer irrigate, no longer get to slop and muck through irrigation water. Now, I wake at five thirty every Monday morning and drive south an hour down Queens Point Road into the hills and jack pines of the Bull Mountains, where I work another man's ranch. I stay the week in a redone homesteader's cabin. All week I fix fence and spray weeds and trail cattle—but he puts up some dryland hay, too. And come haying season it's my job to pull the hay rake behind the ancient Ford tractor, some sixty years old and one of the earliest tractors to have rubber tires, thankfully, which makes

THE BOOK OF WATER

the ride a little easier, though the iron seat is hard as rock and the black stack belches smoke that drifts into my eyes.

It is August, the sun a white hole in the drained sky, and I am so thirsty. I breathe and taste the mineral dust of this high desert country, the ashy tractor smoke. The field ovals the hilltop, which slopes down then into a treeless plain and a dry coulee. On the other side, beyond the cut bank, the land rises into ridge after ridge of wind-carved sandstone. There are no year-round rivers or creeks that run the Bulls—only a rare rain, only a few artesian springs here and there. Now, with a sudden shift of the land, the tractor dips and clatters, nearly throws me from the seat. A moment later, the hay rake hits the same bump and pulls at the coupling pin with a metal-on-metal scream, and the blackbirds rise—I can feel the concussion of their thousand wings—and drift down again to their meal.

I wait until it is nearly unbearable, then kill the tractor and climb onto the four-wheeler and thumb the throttle down and skid and bump as fast as I can over the prairie. I pull up in the shade of a pine and get down on my knees at the muddy burble of Fulton's Spring.

I am so thirsty. It seems I'm always thirsty.

I put my lips to the puddle, to the rotting mass of pine needles and black mud, and drink.

IN THE 1920s, over sixty thousand thirsty farmers left Montana with dusty boots and broken hearts—at least that's what Mr. Lloyd tells me and the other half-dozen farmer's kids in his Montana history class. We laugh, call the quitters candy-asses. Someone boasts that it takes a meaner breed than most to make it out on the Big Dry, that it doesn't matter if rain doesn't follow the plow when you're smart as a coyote and tough as a jackrabbit. Mr. Lloyd shakes his head, his long hair swaying about his bearded face.

THE MOUNTAIN AND THE FATHERS

Mr. Lloyd is a Democrat, like my mother, but he doesn't know how to lay low or stay out of trouble. He eats his sprout sandwiches in front of everyone in the teachers' lounge, wears sandals so you can see his toes. And in class he keeps messing with our myths. He tells us that Burton K. Wheeler, a labor activist and politician who was long known as Bolshevik Burt, was the greatest Montanan that ever lived. He calls Montana a colony for outside interests and shows us pictures of the mountain they turned inside out over in Butte. Half the town fell in that hole, he says. And now the water at the bottom is so toxic it'll kill any bird that lands on it. He points at us and with a flourish finishes, saying, "Federal giveaways and BLM land are the only thing keeping your farms afloat. You aren't so tough. You're just dying slower than most!"

I kind of like Mr. Lloyd. Sometimes, listening to one of his lectures, I will even forget to throw a wad of paper back at whoever threw it at me, or maybe I will absentmindedly mention something we read in class later at lunch and my friends will look at me and turn away. It doesn't help that Mr. Lloyd is not an especially good teacher. He can never find anyone's paper and falls asleep at his desk. He's fired midway through the school year, and he walks on home in his sandals that last day and, the story goes, lies down on his couch and rolls and smokes a joint and leaves it burning in an ashtray near the curtains. Then he packs his things and leaves.

Hours after he has left, the sky midnight black and cold, the house he rents near the swimming pool goes up in flames.

I HEAVE a shovelful of dirt at the flames dancing up the pine.

There is an explosion. Despite my shoveling, the tree has topped out—the whole great, branchy crown of it flowering with fire—and the wind and heat drive me back. I stumble, taste earth and ash. I scramble up and spit.

Someone yells something about needing more shovels on the ridge. I don't know who it is that's yelling. I don't know who anyone is anymore. I am a few weeks back from college, working again this summer on that same dryland Bull Mountain ranch. This morning my boss and I were the only men out on the fire, but the flames have spread fast. Whenever I turn around now there is some new body—sweat-streaked and ash-smudged, working a shovel.

I hear the yelling again. Again about the ridge. Through the smoke, I see the piney ridge some ways in front of me. I am trying to get there. I am trying. I trip on a root or a rock, fall to my knees. I am on my hands and knees in the dirt.

But now there is someone very near me—a sure hand on my shoulder, the metal rim of a canteen at my lips, and a voice, saying, "Here, lean your head back."

I do. I close my eyes and drink. The water is warm and tastes of earth and river rock, is somehow just sweet—like wild plums or chokecherries. I think I have never had something so good. I drink and breathe. I cough, water running down my chin. The canteen slips from my lips. I open my eyes.

I'm sitting on my ass in the dirt in the middle of a forest fire. I am alone. I rise, move toward the fire-bright ridge.

HE IS sitting in an easy chair in his old house near the foothills of the Beartooth Mountains. His breath comes in hitches and gasps. He is so pale. He puts his hand on my hand. My hand a young man's hand now; his a brittle, blown leaf.

He coughs, says, "I don't believe I'll go to the water anymore. I tried, but there was nothing left in it for me. You see, when he died—Walt, that is, your daddy—I lost what it was that I had there." He tells me this, and then, after a minute's pause, he tells me again.

My father has been dead for many years, and Pa Peters still grieves. He and I have had this conversation, or some variation of it, every time I've seen him since the funeral. He looks at me now with his washed-out eyes, coughs again, and says, "I always thought of him as my boy, you know, and he's gone, has been for a while. But you were his boy, see, so I want you to have my fishing gear. It's around here somewhere. Take what you want. I don't need it. I don't have it left in me. I won't go to the water anymore."

So this is what I will do about thirst and fire:

I will rise and walk the dirt path to the river, pull off my shirt and boots and pants, pile them beneath a tangle of willows. I will slip out of my boxer shorts and set them too in the buzzing shade.

With the river at my thighs and my back to the current, I will sit down. The chill like a blow to the chest, I will lean anyway back and back— until water rushes just below my chin. I will place the heels of my hands against the rocky bottom, dig my feet into the gravel, and close my eyes. I will lay my whole self down: river over my face and chest, roaring in my ears, that cold taste of stone on my lips.

I will open my eyes: the pines, the mountains, the rippling sky.

All the world: water.

COAL FURNACE

WHAT YOU DO is open slowly the thick furnace door, for just as soon as it is cracked, the coal fire roars and a breath of oily smoke rushes out.

Once that first burst of heat has subsided, you take a great, long metal tool—which has a looped handle on one end and another hand-hold in the middle that you twist to open and close the claw on the far end—and reach into the fire and claw up and lift the clinkers, the tortuous looking byproducts of burnt coal, and drop them one by one into the ash can, a black and rusting metal bucket in front of the furnace. Then, your face and hands and neck washed with dry heat, you hang the claw back up and take a thin, long-handled shovel and scoop up what loose ash you can, though much of it lifts and rolls and eddies in the fire's twisting wind, and shovel the ash too into the can. You thankfully re-latch the furnace door and breathe a moment and in the crook of your arm wipe your ashy, blasted face.

But you are not done.

Now you pick up the ash can by its handle—careful not to let the hot bottom bump against your legs—and climb the basement stairs and shoulder your way out the front door, the cold October wind suddenly in your lungs, and haul the bucket on out to the gravel road, where you dump the still-burning clinkers and ash in a rut, cinders leaping and wheeling and finally settling.

In the twilight, for it is usually before dinner when you clean the furnace, you look back to the house, with its lit windows and coal smoke slipping out the chimney, and you know it is warm in there and good, and you understand something then of ash and necessity. You understand a coal furnace gives a cheap, if smoky, heat; that one day the ruts of the road will fill with coal clinkers; that the world works like this: You shovel a pickup load of coal, you clean the furnace, you empty the ash cans—and you and yours stay warm.

Though this is what you want, is absolutely what you want, you stare at the dying glow of the clinkers, the cold wind at your ears and wrists, and the stark fact of it shivers and braces you.

A Fragment from My Grandfather's Body

BEFORE THE SUN

"YOUR DAD AND I had a deal. He was going to take charge of the whole place in a few years. And he knew how to do things right. All these ranchers around here selling off their land—not your dad. He would have kept it up and made it pay."

We are driving out into the distances of the Big Dry, and my grandfather is lecturing again. He sits forward in the bench seat and scans the coulees and hills as we rumble over miles of dirt road. I lean into the passenger side door and watch ropes of dust rock across the truck floor. Now and then I steal glances at him: cowboy hat cocked back on his head, his dark and whiskered face, meaty hands flexed, swinging the black wheel. As we near the camp house, he shifts Old Blue into low and lunges through Willow Creek in a splash of mud and stagnant water. A hard spring storm tore the bridge out years ago. Now there is this sudden chasm, the banks washed bare and clean.

My grandfather is seventy-five, and I am eleven, and we are going out again—in this endless prairie ceremony—to fix the many miles of fence that ribbon his six-thousand-acre cattle ranch. He has told me many times that this was the ranch he saved for as he cowboyed under another man's brand through the sun and dust of the Comanche Flats, the ranch he dreamed of as he hauled one-hundred-pound sacks of wheat, one in each hand, through the long nights of harvest at the string of grain elevators he worked in Wheat Basin, Billings, and Dutton. Today, he eyes me and spits, says his own father was a bootlegger and gambler, hard on his wife and harder on his kids, a man who never owned an acre he didn't neglect, letting the cattle overgraze and the fences fall and always losing it in a poker game. He tells me he swore he'd do things differently when he was a man—do right by his family, do right by his land—and that by 1954 he had saved enough money to buy these nine sections of pasture and build a camp house near the banks of Willow Creek. He registered the Lazy Shamrock as his brand, to please his Irish wife, and a few years later bought the three hundred acres of crop land along the Musselshell River that we live on now. He tells me how he worked hard and kept the books and made it all pay time and again, raising up his family and eventually seeing all four of his kids go off to college and make their own way in the world—and how when the work got to be too much, all this land a might lonely, he made a deal for the hay farm with his son-in-law and brought his daughter and her family back to Montana.

I know all these things, this story of the ranch, my grandfather's ranch. I have heard it told many times, and though my grandfather is meanly proud of each turn of the tale, I know that now it is bittersweet for him—for he did raise his children right, did send them off to college, and now his sons live hours and hours away and have no desire to come back to the ranch. Somewhere deep in me I have as well a sense, a bit of blood knowledge, that this place, where Willow Creek arcs and tumbles through the soap-clean smell of sage, is my grandfather, and he is this place—and in the long years of watching neighbors fail and sons leave, he has come to believe the only man besides himself that he could ever trust to run it right was my father, my dead father.

The sun blisters in the sky. We stretch the wires tight against the posts and clamp them down. We eat lunch and walk mile after mile. By late afternoon, we're covered in dust. My grandfather slaps at his jeans and breathes deep. As the sun slips behind the far blue mountains, we drive the gravel road home.

It is only a few months later that my mother sits us down at the kitchen table and tells us that my grandfather has sold the ranch. Without letting anyone know, not his sons or his daughter, my grandfather has up and sold the family ranch, keeping only a few acres to run a small bunch of cattle on. No one knows what to say. In their various absences, and the various guilts those absences have sired, my uncles call and call. My mother cries and cries, then puts our alfalfa fields up for lease as well. Everyone, it seems, is heartbroken.

Except for me. No one—least of all my grandfather, who asks every day about my grades in school and what I'm reading and tells me to study harder—would have made me take the ranch, yet I might have done it, or my brother might have done it, out of some unreasoning and sacred sense of duty, out of misplaced grief. But now—now my grandfather has freed me. So I read and read and fall in love with worlds I have never even seen. I make plans to travel, talk earnestly about the merits of various colleges and universities, as if we have the money to send me to any of them, any of them at all, and my grandfather watches as different men sign the lease papers and take their shot at making it on our hay farm. He notes if they keep up the fences, if they make it to the fields before the sun, and when they move on—they always move on—he shakes his head.

"Your dad would of had those ditches scraped in April and the first cutting up by May," he says, and drives out, with a load of brand-new steel posts, green and gleaming in the dawn light, to fix fence on what bit of land he has left.

PRAYER

GOD IS A small man: pear-shaped, dark-haired, a bit of scraggly beard at his chin. From a light-shot cloud he slumps and judges, raises up his hands now and again, vestments swimming around his wrists: white alb, clover-colored amice, gold stole.

I know the words because I am one of the altar boys, because before mass either John Bergin or my brother or I must help the priest dress in the dark, unfinished room in the back of the church, where the floor is stone and every corner thick with dust-heavy spiderwebs. Our Lady of Mercy is not much more than an outbuilding with a foundation—no plumbing, the heater coughing to a stop, even a light wind fairly rattling the faded stained glass—but it's okay because we are just a mission, the kind of church they have in Africa or Ecuador, and we have mass only once or twice a month. Maybe thirteen or fourteen people show up. There is the Bergin family, all seven of them, big-hipped and freckled. Sandy and Cleora Russell, married so long they look both like bent cottonwood trees along the river. Wooden-legged Matt Kanta. Hatchet-faced Tony Franzel. Sometimes even the beautiful Laird girl, with her jangly silver earrings and Wrangler jeans.

And the priest. Whichever one we happen to have. Priests don't last long out here on the prairie. One, I remember, had a lift and lilt to his voice everyone said was Irish. One couldn't say his consonants right and for his trying, white flecks of spittle built at his lips. One's face was thin and sad. One was very fat and red as beets. When I tell my mother now what God looks like, she whispers no. She says that was just a priest we had here years and years ago. She looks at me with far-off eyes, says, "I'm surprised you remember. That was back when your father was alive."

Today was John Bergin's day to hold the cup and sit up front with the priest. So, today, I pray in back with my family, all of us kneeling on the wooden pew, that little ache in my knees that tells me I am doing what I am supposed to be doing, though I am supposed to keep my eyes closed, too, supposed to find God in the dark, yet I can't help but sneak some looks around: little brother's round, bowed head; older sister with her long hair about her face; and mother, tears slipping silently down her cheeks.

We pray. Even after the host has slicked to nothing on my tongue, even after mass is over and everyone has risen to sip bad coffee and hem and gripe about the weather, we pray. Pray to God with his funny chin beard. Pray to head-hung, bleeding Jesus. Pray to Mother Mary old and alone. Pray to the angels, the communion of saints, all the dear-departed souls who have gone before us. Father, gone before us.

Father, send rain. Father, send sister to a good college. Father, send new high-top Nikes for basketball. Father, why is it I don't remember you? I guess I remember God, but I don't remember you.

Anyway, go ahead and make me as good as mother says you were. Make me a hard worker, an antelope hunter, a trout fisher, a drinker, a dancer, a talker, a thinker, a good-time joke teller.

Father, you are all these but never a father.

IV.

From ranches of isolation

and the busy griefs,

Raw towns that we believe

and die in . . .

—W. H. AUDEN

SKY

WE RODE INTO the world in the backs of pickups.

Say sitting atop what's left of a load of Bull Mountain furnace coal, my jeans blackening and greasy, my grandfather turning his Ford down the gravel road to our house, splitting this load of coal like the last one between his stone cellar and our earthen cellar.

Maybe coming back from the ranch, my grandparents up front and my brother and me in the bed with our backs up against the cab, some old wooden posts and a thick-ringed chain beneath us, the highway wind wheeling dust and straw.

Or letting the GMC idle in the snow-swept north pasture, clambering into the back and cutting twine and tossing a good ton or two of alfalfa hay flake by flake to the sheep—their snorty breaths huffing out their snouts, our labored breaths slipping out our mouths, and the winter-condensed exhaust clouding from the rusted tailpipe.

Or the backs of our thighs burning against the tailgate as my mother drives us all down to the river for an afternoon splash and mud fight.

Or a bunch of boys piling into the bed of my dun-orange '69 GMC for a ride down to the Lacy JC for Gatorades and beef jerky before basketball practice.

Or Tony and Chip—who seemed even as boys so certain the world would not ruin them, or perhaps they simply welcomed whatever ruin might come—squirming out the back window of the cab and climbing into the pickup bed at sixty miles an hour, shaking cans of Mountain Dew and tossing them back of us like bombs onto the highway.

Or the river-loud night my friend drank too much up at that summer basketball tournament in Reedpoint. We were in the junior high division, on a team with some boys we'd played against during the last season, and after we lost out, one of their older brothers told us to jump into the back of his sleek little Toyota pickup, and we did, and he drove us then up into the Absaroka Mountains, where there was a fire of pine and cedar spitting hot sap and sparks, a radio turned up loud, cans of Bud Light and a bottle of vodka going around and around. We couldn't have been more than fourteen. We'd been friends since third grade—though in a few months his mother, scared for her life, would leave in the middle of the night with him and his sisters and we would lose touch.

That night out of Reedpoint, shoulder to shoulder in the pickup bed—where I'd made him lie down after he'd pulled on that bottle one too many times—my friend told me he wished his father would just die, that God was asleep at the wheel up there letting a son of a bitch like his father live, that it would be a whole lot easier if someone would just murder the bastard.

And for the mountains and tall pines and ragged firelight, I couldn't even see the sky.

BRUCE WHEARTY

IF SOME BOYS start messing around, he doesn't look the other way or shake his finger—he throws them up against the wall. And not just the bad ones. He'll take the good boys who are being bad only right then and throw them up against the wall, too. He'll throw just about any boy up against the wall and hold him there by the armpits or with bunched fistfuls of winter coat, the boy's sneakered feet swinging just above the blacktop, and Mr. Whearty—his dark beard wild about his face; his black, thick-rimmed glasses framing his wide eyes; and that smell of him, of earth and burnt coffee and prairie weeds, of someone who lives half the year in a tepee down on the Musselshell River and doesn't use deodorant and doesn't care—he'll say, "Tell me what you did, and why it was wrong, and then you can go."

Folks around town shake their heads, claim that Mr. Whearty is a hippie, a tree hugger, a radical. But my mother—who doesn't wear makeup herself; who, even though our turntable is broken and we don't have the money to fix it, every now and again gets out her old Joan Baez and Gordon Lightfoot records and runs her hands across those worn, dusty covers—tells me that folks around here only call

Mr. Whearty those names because they don't know what else to call him, don't know anyone like him.

I think maybe my mother's right. Sure, Mr. Whearty writes letter after letter to the president. Sure, he refuses to watch TV. But he cuts and stacks cords of pinewood outside his tepee, and he stays as warm as the rest of us all winter. And you should see him teach. There's no I'm-okay-you're-okay nonsense. He simply will not abide students putting their heads down on their desks during algebra. He makes us turn in our homework first thing every morning. He has us analyze stories and poems, has us deliver, in front of the whole class, the speeches of Abraham Lincoln and Chief Joseph and Martin Luther King Jr. And he will especially not allow for tardiness, bullying, or dishonesty.

This is all news to us. We have only just finished with dioramas and clay models as major educational undertakings. Mr. Whearty doesn't care. He has a chart and makes us read real books, lots of them. He has us perform *Macbeth* for the whole school up on the main stage. When Halloween comes around, he dresses up like a pancreas. He just doesn't care. Or maybe it's that he does care.

Mr. Whearty plans a Squid Fest, complete with squid dissection, squid feast, and interpretive squid dance. There is a squid-trivia competition, too, which I win, which makes me the Squid King. I am proud to be the Squid King. And Mr. Whearty is proud of me—but not too proud. He still makes me work. He pushes me from bright-covered fantasy paperbacks to Tolkien and LeGuin, hands me *A Tree Grows in Brooklyn* and *A River Runs Through It*. I read them all, I read and read and, like Mr. Whearty, do not apologize for it. In fact, I begin to glory in it. I get as smart and weird as I want, and I don't care what the other kids think.

Today, though, I have lost my book. I was reading Steinbeck, *Of Mice and Men*. I liked it. I didn't mean to lose it. I don't know what's happened to it. And because my face goes bright and hot at even the thought of doing something wrong, I have been for most of the morning trying to figure out how to tell Mr. Whearty the truth and still stay out of trouble. Maybe, I decide, it's a matter of presentation. So, when we sit down for our one-on-one reading session, I fold my hands in my lap and say, clearly, as if there is no other way to put it, "My book was lost."

"No," Mr. Whearty says.

I feel like I might fall out of my chair. I start to sputter.

"You lost it," he says, cutting me off. "It was not just lost, as if you are not responsible, as if it had the power of locomotion. It is a book. It is not animate. It did not get up and go hide from you. No. You are responsible. You lost it. Tell me that you lost it."

Mr. Whearty has never said anything like this to me before. I mean, I was the Squid King. I blink back tears, mumble, "I lost it."

"Yes, you did. But we'll find you another copy." He rises to leave but looks down at me again. "And don't use the passive voice. It's sloppy. It confuses subject and object, and then we no longer understand action. You know better than that. Don't do it."

As Mr. Whearty walks away, I stare, shamed, at my shoes.

And when at the end of the year the school board sort of encourages Mr. Whearty to leave, and he does, I pretend I'm as happy as all those boys he threw up against the wall, and then all summer long, and through the next school year, and the year after that, laughing in the lunchroom or making fun of the one kid who gets picked behind me in PE, I keep trying to convince all of them, and myself, I'm just like everyone else.

ED DEMPSEY

MY GRANDFATHER LEANS out the pickup window and says he'll be having coffee at the Lazy JC. "And Ed," he adds. "Try not to scare the boy."

Ed sucks at his teeth, eyes me up and down. "Jim, I can't promise a thing."

My grandfather grins and drives away. Ed waves me around the corner of the house, and we weave through a sloping dirt yard spotted with tough bunchgrass and variously arranged piles of bolts and rebar and blown tires and old two-cycle engines and finally make our way up to a windowless, tin-roofed shed slumped near the barbed wire of the back fence. He yanks on the strap of hide stapled to the door—the gray boards biting into the dust, the clanking knock of steel chains and wood from somewhere inside—and even for his age and bulk, Ed slips gracefully into the dark yawn of shadow he's opened between the shed door and the shed. After a moment, I follow.

What light there is falls thinly from the cracks and knots in the boards. Motes of dust hover and spin in each wedge and shaft. The air feels ancient, tastes of rot and spice. The floor, like the yard, is hardpan dirt, a few pale weeds twisting for the light. The ceiling is just high enough for a man to straighten himself, and the clanking, I can see now, comes from the rows and rows of steel traps hung along the walls: the slender curves of number ones like the wings of sparrows; solid number threes; the massive, menacing jaws of number sixes, like the jaws of what they snare: bear.

Ed Dempsey is big as a bear, but slumped and pudgy and bald. He has turned his big body away from me, is studying the rows of shelves along the far wall. He takes a long time. I stare at the stubbly back of his neck, his shoulders rising with breath. He must be remembering, for the shelves are not labeled, and neither are the glass bottles that crowd each shelf: some green, some brown, some purple, some with droppers for lids, some with burnt driftwood corks. I imagine he enjoys remembering, I imagine there is a story that explains each one, which ridge and what kind of coyote and how the rain came. These are Ed's blue-glass stories, these bottles and vials he considers—first this one and then that one, the glass clinking like small bells as he thumbs through them. I don't care how long this takes, how long he spends remembering. I'll wait, because for Christmas my grandfather gave me three good steel traps and a half-dozen snares. Two of the traps are number ones, and I have caught quite a few prairie dogs with them—but prairie dogs are easy, will practically fall into a trap, sniff out and tangle themselves in a snare. My other trap is bigger, a number three, and I have set it where my grandfather told me to set it, along a dry wash up north. I am hoping for a coyote because a coyote is legitimate, something to pelt out and brag about. My grandfather has trapped mountain lion and lynx before, but even he says coyotes are hard to catch. They're sneaky, wise. And coyotes are a sheep rancher's devilment. Unchecked, they'll thin a lamb crop down to nothing in just a few months. So, beyond a fine gray-red pelt, my trapping will matter, will be something I can be proud of—and that's why I'm here. Though my grandfather has trapped a fair number in his time, he is no maker of potions. He too came to Ed, or before him Buster Knapp, for the promise of a dark glass bottle, for a tincture squeezed from the pea-sized glands of a coyote and mixed with rabbit piss and cow's blood and left to ferment for a good thirty years.

Ed takes up a small brown bottle now and holds it to the light, twists off the cap and gives it a sniff. He holds it out to me. I sniff too. It smells of wet fur and oranges and what I think is sex. I would like to keep smelling it, but Ed pulls it back and caps it and wraps it in burlap and hands it to me, saying, "What you do is you break yourself open a bone, any bone, and dribble some of this in the hollow—just a drop or two, now—and then set that bone right at the edge of a cut bank. You've got your trap set on a cut bank, right? Or a dry wash? Right, okay then, set it right at the edge, just past your trap—maybe in a sagebrush or something where it's hard to see or get to—and you by golly ought to have yourself a coyote come morning."

I nod and thank him and step out into the blinding white light. Ed follows, pulling the wooden door shut and wrapping the length of hide tight around the nail. We make our way back up to the house, a two-story that like most houses in town has seen better days. Ed, too, is old and past his body's best work. He has a wife who stays shut up in the house. I don't know if he has any children. If he does, they don't live around here and I don't know their stories. Yet unlike most of the washed-up cowboys, farmers who've had to sell, and other has-beens, in his old age Ed has gone and taken on another life. Ed Dempsey is the mayor of Melstone. Though after work in this dark shed Ed still milks the bladders of skunks and muskrats, he spends his days dealing with school levies and zoning laws and forms in triplicate. I don't ask him about this, don't ask him how he reconciles these two lives. Don't ask him about the way I hope for nothing so much as to trap a coyote, to steady the rifle at my shoulder, and as the coyote snaps and gnashes at its own bone-raw and bloody leg, shoot it cleanly in the head. Or why the other day, after finishing another Steinbeck novel, *Tortilla Flat*, I felt somehow bigger than myself and kindly toward all the world.

I don't ask him about any of these things I cannot seem to reconcile. I shake his hand. I say, "Thanks," and make my way down the gravel road to the general store.

And no one but Ed Dempsey knows I'm carrying in my pocket a glass bottle of magic.

KELLY DEMPSEY

WHEN WE COME into town for a gallon of strawberry ice cream and a bag of Doritos, the Lazy JC is all closed up, so my brother and I jog over to the Sportsman Bar, where we know we'll find Kelly Dempsey, who keeps the after-hours keys.

The Sportsman is one of Melstone's last grand brick false-fronts. Forty years ago, you would have found a whole high-shouldered row of them. First, the Antlers, the little rooms on the second floor littered with the silk stockings of whores, then the Wilson Hotel, Herron's, the Grant, the Sportsman, and the U.S. post office—though all but the Sportsman and the post office have been torn down or boarded up. Weedy lots and busted windows line Main Street now. The Snakepit, the only other bar in town, is along the highway in a cheap prefab building that also houses the only café in the hundred-mile stretch of Highway 12 between Roundup and Forsyth. The café serves the usual flash-frozen fries and preformed hamburger patties, and the Snakepit is the kind of bar where a shot means schnapps, where light beer and wine coolers fill the fridge. Not the Sportsman. Beer comes in a squat can there, and a shot means pick your whiskey. The house special, one of the few things besides peanuts you can get to eat at all, is a grease-soaked paper bag of hard-fried chicken gizzards.

So, it's something to be just fifteen, still a boy, really—though now you can drive into town with your brother and are allowed to stay up late and eat ice cream and Doritos and watch reruns of *Night Court* and *M*A*S*H* and the half hour of music videos they show every Friday night on channel 4—and be stepping up to the heavy wooden door of the Sportsman Bar, pushing that very door open.

The air is smoky and close. A battered pool table shines beneath the glare light of a bare bulb. Beer posters featuring bikinied, big-haired women draped over muscle cars hang from the walls. A bookshelf stuffed with paperback westerns and yellowed romances rests near the woodstove in the corner. Country music drifts from a dusty radio on a high shelf behind the bar. Though the long antenna is flagged with tinfoil, whirrups of static snap through the jangling music. On the same shelf sits a small black-and-white television, the screen shifting and flickering without sound. And every table in the place is empty. The men—for they are all men here at the Sportsman—sit on tall stools at the bar. Their cowboy hats and ball caps pulled low, their elbows heavy on the bar lip, bellies sagging beneath. They look at us and do not look at us—a kind of slow, sideways glance. They tip their beer cans to their mouths, wipe their mustaches with the backs of their shirtsleeves.

From back of the bar, fist on her good hip, Maureen looks us up and down. Maureen owns the Sportsman and is ancient and cantankerous and broad-shouldered and big as any of the men. "Boys," she says, in a voice that means our answer must be good, "what do you need in here?"

"Is Kelly around?" my brother asks.

There is a beat of silence. I attempt to clarify. "To open the store. For ice cream." Immediately I wish I hadn't said a thing. I seem always to be doing this: saying the wrong thing, not understanding that the rules here are hard and fast about what a boy can say and what he is not supposed to say, what a boy can do and not do—if he is to make a man anyway.

Thankfully no one laughs or snorts. No one says a thing. Not even Maureen. She just turns back to the TV and points to the man slumped at the end of the bar.

His back has been to us. We didn't recognize him. But as he turns on his stool we see it is Kelly: hair in greasy tufts beneath his ball cap, the few teeth left in his head a dull yellow in the black of his half-open mouth, his face and neck pitted and lined and heavily whiskered, his skin the dull, burnt color of red earth. His snap shirt has come untucked, and his ripped jeans are fraying here and there, his cowboy boots shit-splattered and deeply creased.

Kelly grins at us, his lips like a jagged wound. He's winged his elbows back behind him, to steady himself on the bar, and because he is so drunk and slumped and small—easily the smallest man here—the bar lip hits him at his shoulders, which makes him seem even smaller: He looks like a boy of sorts, underfed and overworked but with eyes bright as the cinder of a cigarette.

Brothers are the same, and they are different. Kelly is Ed Dempsey's younger brother. Ed is the mayor; Kelly is a drunk. Ed is a big, heavy man, and he lives in a two-storied house. Kelly can't be much more than 120 pounds soaking wet, and he lives in a camper-trailer set up on blocks. But both carry the name Dempsey. My brother, though a year younger, is taller than I am, and graceful and sure on the basketball court. He knows pickups, too, and horses, and whose land is whose as we drive by on the highway. I'm not much more than hopeless with a basketball, and though I've read nearly every book in the school library, I don't know half the things my brother does. I wonder what it means for us. I have heard that when Kelly was a boy his father beat him, with switches and boards, with his hands. I have heard that one day Ed stood up for Kelly, stood up to their raging father. Kelly sits here in the Sportsman Bar now working his tongue over his toothless gums, and I am sure that day he hated his brother for it.

"Ice cream," Kelly says, his voice all bark and growl. "Boys got to have their ice cream. Just let me finish this here cigarette." He takes a deep drag and smoke drifts out his mouth and turns and hangs at his hat brim. "Say, which one of you's which? I can't ever tell the damn difference."

Kelly should know us. In the years after my father died, Kelly often worked out at our place. He hadn't known my father. He'd just gotten back from twenty years in North Dakota and needed work. He irrigated, vaccinated sheep, fixed fence for us, cursing a blue streak the whole time. He was half-drunk most of the time, too, and as a result didn't do an especially good job. When our alkaline water finally ate through the kitchen faucet, Kelly installed a new one, though he mixed up the hot and cold, and both knobs turn backward. But Kelly just kept coming back, and because he'd take a paycheck my mother felt better about it. Even now, after Ed has gotten him a job with the city, after Kelly has started helping at the Lazy JC, after we have leased out our ranch, he keeps coming back. He'll drive on up in his rusty wreck of a pickup and stomp up the porch stairs and ask our mother what she needs done.

My brother begins to speak, but Kelly cuts him off. "Hell, I guess don't tell me. I haven't remembered yet. I won't remember now. You look so damn much alike anyways." He says this and smacks his lips and laughs, but keeps looking right at us, as if studying us.

We shift on our feet, look around the barroom. The other men concentrate on their beers. They crunch peanuts in their fists and drop the shells in the brass spittoons at their feet. Maureen scowls at the television.

"Hell," Kelly says again, loudly, and stands, his stool scraping and knocking against the wood floor. "I guess we'll go on over. Don't want to keep you waiting. Don't want to do you like your mother does me. I mean, don't you boys think it's about goddamn time she falls in love with me like she ought to?"

My brother flinches. My face goes hot. The men at the bar turn ever so slightly our way.

"What do you say, boys? You think maybe your mom and me?" Kelly brings again his cigarette to his lips—brings it to his lips slowly, carefully, and closes his mouth around it and smokes.

Once, maybe six months after my father died, an old friend of my mother's took us all to the Sheraton Hotel in Billings, which according to local lore was the tallest building between Minneapolis and Seattle. My brother and I were silly with excitement. This man had two boys, too—I think he was divorced—and we played in the pool with his boys most of the day. Later, we all went to dinner together and ate thick steaks and shrimp and things like that. He wore glasses and was a wheat farmer. We all talked and had a good time. I think I liked him.

We were in our pajamas, the four of us boys trying to decide what to watch on television, when my mother came and got my brother and me and made us pack up our things. Though we didn't ask, she kept telling us it wasn't turning out how she thought. We left and drove the eighty miles home in the dark. Since then she has been my mother, and my brother's mother, and my sister's mother, even though my sister is off now at college. My mother is a teacher, too, and she reads and prays and sometimes cries to herself—but now this puny, filthy son of a bitch Kelly Dempsey tells me she is a woman.

Of course she is a woman. I know that, but I still feel ashamed, wronged. Like I should do something. My brother isn't doing anything, and I'm not doing anything, and the men at the bar are looking at us, full on now, waiting for us. I guess we ought to tell him to go straight to hell. We ought to hit him in his rotten mouth. We ought to lay into him with curses and fists. That's what these men would do, that's what they've done.

We don't. We stand there moonfaced and dumb. Bile rises invisibly from our guts, rises into our throats, rises and burns—and is still burning when some few weeks later we drive to Billings and buy Pearl Jam albums and pierce our ears, when we come home wearing baggy jeans and black Doc Martens, lank hair hanging in our eyes. We stand here in the Sportsman Bar silent as pines, but we burn. We are the fatherless sons of a mother. We will burn and court the daughters of the drunks and fathers of Melstone. We will remain boys. We will hold tight to the lovely idiocy and burning freedom of boys.

Kelly stubs out his smoke and reaches for his keys. "Shit, boys, I'm just fucking around with you. Come on. Let's get some ice cream."

For his slight weight, his bootfalls fairly echo across the floor.

DOM BARSILUCCI

WE ARE STANDING in a rough circle on the crumbling sidewalk
outside the Sportsman Bar, spitting now and again and cursing this
teacher or that teacher and drinking Mountain Dew. Someone pulls
out a can of Copenhagen and packs it tight with a quick flick of his
wrist and passes it around, and we all take a pinch and stuff it in our
lip because, more than anything, we are trying to act cool—though
being so far from everything we see on television, so far out on the
prairie that most of us can't get more than one television station, none
of us is sure what cool is or isn't. We are mostly boys, save Megan,
Tony's sister, who wears her Wranglers tight and her strawberry hair
in curls around her face. I have a terrible crush on Megan and so am
trying to act the coolest of all, which means I am standing unnaturally
still and saying next to nothing.

But now the door of the Sportsman swings wide, the little bell
clanging, and old Dom Barsilucci steps drunkenly out into our circle. He stands there a moment and grins, wheezes, lights a cigarette. Smoke slips from between his lips, rockets out the wing-like
nostrils of his nose. I know Dom the way I know most everyone in

town—which is to say I have maybe in my entire life said one or two words to him but know anyway that he was a star basketball player in high school; that his youngest son was knifed in a bar fight and thrown in the Yellowstone River years ago; that, after drinking for weeks on end, he'll sometimes see snakes crawling out his ears and all over him; that he'll yell and slap and thrash, though there's nothing at all in the world there.

So that's Dom, with his saloon-lazy eyes and gin-sloppy smile, the ridiculous way he just lets his cigarette ride the shift of his lips, never taking it between his fingers, never ashing it, just drawing the smoke in and in. And now Tony is grinning, getting ready to poke some fun at drunk old Dom, and Megan—her hair slick and shining in the glare of the town's two or three buzzing streetlights—is grinning as well, looking from Tony to Dom and back again to Tony, and this means, I am sure, that I have lost her. As long as things were boring and ordinary, I had some hope, for then—I'd imagined, anyway—I might have stood out: my almost good looks, my quiet thoughtfulness, my long-suffering-but-noble adoration of her.

"Hey, Barstoolie," Tony calls, "seen any snakes lately?"

"Nope," Dom says and smacks his lips. "But a drawbridge went up on me the other day—and sploosh! I was in the river!"

Tony is the first to laugh. He points right at Dom and laughs. I laugh, too. We all do. Dom just turns in the circle of us, says, "Now, you little green-nutters remember what to do if you get hungry out there on the prairie? You remember, right?"

We shake our heads.

"Hell, you eat a cow pie and chew on a sagebrush!"

Smoke billows from his half-open mouth. He looks more than drunk: He looks unmoored, lost, drowned. But I guess it's hilarious, because we are all laughing, saying, "Sounds good, Dom. Will do! You bet!"

But Dom stops turning. He's staring right at me. "What the hell are you doing out here, boy? Out here with me and the peanut gallery? You ought to be home studying or something. Well? What the hell?"

I don't say anything. I'm trying to watch Tony, hoping to take my cues from him and play this all off as part of the joke, but Dom moves in even closer to me. I can't see around him. His breath is hot and vinegary. I grin, hoping that everyone thinks this is somehow funny.

"I'm serious, boy," Dom says, straightening up, snapping his cigarette to the gravel. "I knew your father. I know your mother. Talk about a good man. And a lady. You got to do right by them. Right by yourself."

He says this, blows smoke out his nose, and steps back into the bar.

WARREN MAXWELL

WE ARE IN the night shadows of cottonwoods.

Bare branches fracture moonlight across our faces. The wind comes at us twisting and hard. As we shiver and shift, the dry stems of bunchgrass rasp and crack beneath us.

It is early winter and we are in a draw that slopes down to a dusty, nameless, alkaline reservoir off Highway 12 on the way east to the near ghost town of Ingomar, Montana, out on the vast, scabby, wind-scoured plains of the Big Dry proper, where some hundred years ago the last of the buffalo were surrounded and slaughtered, where no rivers run and the homesteaders gave up early and often, where nearly every town the Milwaukee Road seeded has blown away with the dust. It is just Rooster Crawford and me, and we are standing around and hunching our shoulders in the wind and not saying much. We are waiting for someone Rooster knows to bring us a case of beer.

"You think that's him?" I ask, pointing to the pinprick headlights cresting the hill.

"No," Rooster says, and spits, working a wad of Copenhagen around his mouth. "It's too early. You don't take a call at the Jersey

Lily from some kid and then buy a case of beer and leave right away. That'll get your impatient ass caught."

I shove my hands into the pockets of my jeans, stare at the hard-pan dirt beneath me. I don't know why Rooster picked me to come out here with him. Rooster is three years older than me, and though he's not exactly the most popular guy in school, you must anyway reckon with Rooster. Both his parents were rodeo champions, and his grandfather was an early-day cowboy and settler. Rooster himself is slender and strong and starts on the basketball team. He tucks his Garth Brooks–style shirts into his Wranglers and is always giving titty-twisters or sneaking up behind you and slapping the back of your head hard enough to make your teeth ring. Though I'm fifteen now and have mostly graduated from that kind of torment, I still cringe at the way Rooster will key a teacher's car just to key it, the way he always has a rifle or a gun in his truck and will pull it out and point it at you or fire it over your head just for kicks. And I hate most of all the way he shakes his head and sneers at me for not being able to rope and ride and cowboy, as if my very existence offends him, as if no matter what I do I will always be this fumbling, bookish boy. In three years I'll leave for college—as long as I get a scholarship or two, I'm gone—but three years seems a lifetime. Why is it I fit in so miserably here? Why didn't my grandfather ever teach me to rope, to ride? Sometimes, it's almost funny, almost like some cosmic joke—like tonight, when Rooster said he sure as hell wasn't driving halfway out to Ingomar to wait in the cold all by himself and none of the other boys volunteered, and so Rooster pointed at me, told me to get in the truck.

I kick at a sagebrush, work around the gnarled stalk of it with the toe of my tennis shoe. Rooster stands thin and straight, his thumbs hooked in his pockets. His sharp moonlight shadow wings away from him. I envy his certainty—the way at any given moment he seems to know exactly who and where he is. He turns to me now. "You know Warren, your cousin, right?"

"Yeah. I know him." Warren is a shirttail relative of sorts, a child of one of my grandfather's cousins. He used to spend his summer's working for my grandfather, and though he's somewhat younger, my mother remembers him around the ranch. I've only met him a couple of times, but I remember Warren because he left—left his family's place, left Montana altogether. He lives in Minneapolis now. He wears button-up shirts and slacks with a sharp crease down the front, and he shakes your hand and looks you in the eye. He is as sure of himself as any cowboy. To me, Warren is proof that it's possible.

"My uncles went to high school with him, over in Forsyth," Roosters says. "They tell me he was a faggot. A real weird little fucker. Tried to be a hippie and wear his hair long and things like that—but he couldn't hide that he was just queer. He still queer?"

"He's married. He's got kids. I don't think so."

"That don't mean anything. He could still be queer."

"I guess. I don't know. He's really smart. He's a lawyer, works in a skyscraper in Minneapolis. He makes good money."

"He ain't so smart," Rooster says and spits, and then with his thumb and forefinger pinches from his lips a few loose bits of Copenhagen and flicks them away.

"How do you know?"

Rooster eyes me and grins. "It was cold like this, I guess, and they were out having themselves a beer party, and someone dared Warren to jump in the river. So he took off his clothes and did it. When he came out, some boys grabbed him and tied his hands behind his back and lassoed his little peter—pulled the rope tight, so it wouldn't slip—and then threw it up over a big cottonwood limb and tied it off on the other side, tied it tight now, so Warren couldn't even move." Rooster looks straight at me, grinning even wider now, daring me to challenge him. "See, he ain't so smart. They hung him by his pecker."

"Who told you that?" I ask, trying to keep my voice even. "It's probably made up."

"Nope. That's the truth. Some of those boys were my uncles. They've told me that one about a hundred times. They're always telling that one."

"Did they let him go?"

"That's the best part. They took his clothes and left him there. Drove back into town and told everyone. Half the town came out and saw that queer fucker buck naked and strung up by his pecker." Rooster laughs out loud and spits, looks at me like I too should think it's funny as hell. "I guess eventually someone called your grandpa— he was over there in Forsyth for something or other—and he came out and got him down."

I swallow, turn away. I feel I might throw up.

I don't want Rooster to see, to call me a queer, to carry this other story back to town—but something's gotten hold of my heart, my ribs, a great hand tightening down. This shame is so great. I can't even think of Warren, can't think of how he makes it through a day, even so far away. And my grandfather—who I have long known is different than the other old ranchers and cowboys, who bought his part of this country late, who never taught us to ride and rope, who doesn't curse and drink until he's yellow-eyed, who sold his land on his own terms—this is his shame, too. Or is that not right at all? Is it not their shame but their triumph? That they lived through this, didn't let it destroy them, drive them into dereliction and anger? I don't know. I don't know.

I breathe and swallow and take a wobbly step or two toward the dry reservoir. The wind twists again, violently, and the cottonwoods creak and clatter. Moonshot shadows dance.

I don't know, I don't know if I'll make it.

ALL APOLOGIES

JUSTIN BENDS HIMSELF over his beat-up Alvarez, tufts of long blond hair falling across his thin face. *Spring is here again*, he sings, *tender age in bloom, he knows not what it means, sell the kids for food—*.

He's trying hard to gravel up the bottoms, break and scatter the glass each time he hits the top—but his voice is still a boy's sweet voice, and those acoustic chords spill too sweetly too. It doesn't sound like it's supposed to sound, like it sounds spit from the round mouth of the radio. We don't care. We are done with the day's work, are having a cigarette now out back of the school building, the long light stretching the world into warm, windy distances.

It is June, some late afternoon in the year of our Lord 1994. I am sixteen. I have taken a wage job this summer as a janitor's assistant at the school in Roundup, the next town over. I am saving for college.

Justin just showed up earlier this week, and Louie, the head janitor, slapped a screwdriver in his hand and set him up scraping gum off the bottom of the bleachers with me. We didn't talk much. Just eyed each other a bit. He wore ragged cargo pants and a gaping flannel shirt, took cigarette breaks every hour. I kept my T-shirt tucked into my jeans, jeans my mother had laundered fresh that morning, and while he smoked I read for a few minutes from *For Whom the Bell Tolls*. It was the next day—Louie curled on the couch in the teachers' lounge, thrashing, calling out, working his trembling way through another hangover—that I stole the little FM radio that's always supposed to be tuned to KCAT, Cat Country, and flipped it over to KROX 94.1. Oh, those heart-shaking, beatific screams. We were mopping the gym floor. Justin started singing first. He knew all the words. I knew some of them. Soon we were singing and running up and down the gym floor, our mop handles our microphones. It was fun. We sang those bad, sad songs loudly—and when we were done, rather than wake Louie to ask him what to do next, we leaned back on the bleachers and talked. Justin is sixteen, too. Like me, he loves Nirvana and Pearl Jam. He's not saving for college, but a new guitar. And he doesn't have a father either—his not dead but gone.

And this, too: Justin's from Seattle, where the music comes from. I couldn't imagine it. It didn't seem possible. How did he ever end up in eastern Montana? Out on the Big Dry? He shrugged and hopped off the bleachers, told me he thought it was about a couple of months ago, maybe more, that his mom had given him cash enough for a new pair of boots and a bus ticket, told him to call her brother in Montana—and then, like his father, disappeared.

But who cares about gone fathers and piece-of-shit jobs? Now the early summer sun is going big and red in the west, and Louie has headed down to the bar, and Carol, the school secretary, has left as well, and so we are sitting out back of the shop on the bench the teachers use for their own cigarette breaks, smoking and laughing, Justin strumming his guitar and singing. Justin is waiting for his uncle to come pick him up. I have my old GMC pickup here but don't want to leave just yet. This is too good.

I have lived all my life on these Montana plains, and it has somehow never been enough. I know I don't fit very well here—can't cowboy and grin easily at the girls—but it's more than that, too. In the stories my mother and grandfather tell me, in the books I read, there are other ways to live in the world, other worlds. I am wondering if it is okay that I scribble stories on notebook paper and hide them under my bed, wondering if it is okay that I write essays in English class arguing for the necessity of gun control and the moral responsibility of welfare, wondering if it is okay I don't like Garth Brooks and Shania Twain, that I love instead a lonely bass riff and Cobain's cement scream. I am wondering about all these things, and so Justin—his earrings catching the late light, his long hair wild about his face—is a kind of revelation.

There is a half-empty soft pack of Winstons on the dun slats of the bench between us, and the hills have gone some unearthly shade of rust and blue. If I squint a bit, the ragged mountains in the distance look like city spires. And most of all there is the music—the music coming from both our mouths, the music that doesn't sound quite right but anyway good enough, the music that lets us be here and not here, who we are and who we dream we might really be: Montana; Seattle; abandoned, dreaming boys; world-weary, smoke-eating men.

THE DAYS are long and still lengthening, and again we are just off work, barreling down the dust and gravel of the county road to the river. For the past three weeks or so we have been working Saturdays as well and so have spent nearly every hour of the waking day together. It is heady and intense, like fruit brandy or some sugared bourbon, this sudden friendship—and all the more urgent because in the past three weeks I have realized that during the school year it wouldn't be this way. The space we have made and claimed these last weeks wouldn't be allowed. Justin simply wouldn't fit anywhere, and so would spend his days taking apart lawn mower engines in the machine shop, while I'd be in the biology lab; after school, I'd huff up and down the court at basketball practice, while Justin would wander downtown alone, maybe sit on the crumbling sidewalk and smoke. Yet this summer, none of that matters. What matters is we work together, we listen to music together.

At the old iron bridge we skid to a stop and clamber out of the truck and squirm through the space between barbed wire and bridge rails and slide down to the weed-and-gravel bed of the river, where we strip off our shirts and shoes and jump in. Not to swim, really— the river here is too shallow for that—but only to cool down, to be wet awhile in the hot wind.

We have been working in the sun all day today: cutting the front lawn with the coughing push mower, spraying weeds in the side-walk cracks, raking the gravel in the parking lot, and all manner of other ridiculous jobs Louie reserves exclusively for us because Louie came back from Vietnam pissed off; because Louie, like everyone else around here, votes Republican and listens to Rush Limbaugh all hours of the day and thinks boys should keep their hair cut short; because Louie hefts in his two hands the wooden bat he keeps in his truck, tells us it's his hippy-and-nigger stick, and then points it right at us, says, "You boys keep your noses clean. And get your goddamn hair cut."

"Fuck him," Justin says, stepping up onto the bank and lighting a cigarette, rivulets of water still running off him.

I slip again beneath the warm, green-brown water, then break back through the surface and breathe, shake my wet head. "Yeah," I say.

Justin stares at me. "No, no," he says. "Not just, *Yeah*. Say it, Wilkins. Say, *Fuck you, Louie*."

"Why?"

"Just do it."

"I don't get it."

"Christ. Sometimes you're so clueless. You know what Vedder and Cornell and all those guys are singing about? They're singing about *fuck you*. They're not hiding, not trying to fit in or please anyone. If you really believe it, you have to stand by it. So, say it."

For a moment I roll the words around in my mind. I can almost see the disappointment slide across my mother's face. She's a strict Catholic and takes, along with every other part of my upbringing, moral instruction very seriously. "Okay, fine," I say. "Fuck you, Louie."

A smile breaks across Justin's face. He's skinny, his teeth too big—one of the front ones a bit chipped at the bottom—but even cranky Carol has to smile when Justin smiles, like I smile back at him now.

"So," he says, pulling a cigarette out for me as I sit down in the gravel beside him, "tell me one more time: Which ones are hottest? Which ones are nicest? And which ones will still talk to you after they find out you're so fucking poor you have to work as a fucking janitor's assistant all fucking summer?"

I take a deep drag. I don't smoke with him at work, but these days we'll kill a pack between the two of us pretty quickly afterward—out at the dam or up at the oil wells or just driving around. Early on we made some kind of unspoken deal: Cigarettes are his responsibility; gas for the GMC is mine. It's worked out so far. I breathe a bellyful of smoke out over the weeds and water. "Does this mean you're coming to school with me next fall?"

"Christ. School this and school that! Man, I just want to hear about the girls! Just tell me about the goddamn girls!"

"Okay, okay," I say. "Okay."

And he lays down in the dirt and gravel, cigarette clamped tight between his lips, his fingers laced behind his head. And I sit cross-legged, wet hair hanging in my eyes, cigarette smoking between my fingers, and tell him—tell us both, really—about beautiful Gillian Newman, lovely Leak Eike, kind Addie Adams. Stories, too, are my responsibility. Though we always start with the girls, Justin doesn't really care what they're about, just so long as they're good. I talk about books and politics. I tell him my grandfather's tall prairie tales, I tell him my mother's dewy-eyed '60s anecdotes. Sometimes, I tell him about all the places we'll travel, the dark-haired women who will love us. And sometimes, after a story about the way Gillian will smile and ask to borrow your Candlebox CDs or which teachers will take you seriously and which teachers to watch out for, Justin's even said he might want to stay, to start school here—if his uncle will let him, if I'll help him with his homework. It makes me happy when he says this. It is as if my stories have the power to remake this place, make it so someone from a city would want to live here.

Yet I don't tell Justin that my stories aren't about this little town, these plains. Not really. When I tell my stories, things come out brighter, more interesting. This place I make for us is not this place. These few weeks of summer feel already so far away from here, like after work, driving around the scrub hills, we might turn some particular corner and the dust will die down and the glass and steel and steep streets of Seattle will rise suddenly up, the blue water of the bay shimmering in the distance. My stories aren't about what we are. My stories are about what we might be.

After I finish describing in detail what slender Daisy Laird would look like if she traded in Wranglers and rodeo shirts for low-slung army surplus pants and a tight, much-washed Pearl Jam T-shirt, and after Justin finishes convulsing right there in the dust in agony of it all, we light Winstons for the road and pile into the GMC and spin gravel back into town, singing, always singing, *What else should I be? All apologies—*.

IT'S THE middle of another day of shitty outside work, of 110-degree heat and dust and mosquitoes, when from across the parking lot

Justin calls and waves me over to the supply shed. It's near break time, so I kill the weed-eater and set it on the ground, wipe my face with my T-shirt.

By the time I get there, Justin has disappeared inside. I peek in. It's hot and stuffy but at least out of the sun. "What's up?" I ask as my eyes adjust, as I see Justin's face flare in the quick, quavering light of a Bic. Then vanish.

"Pull the door closed," he says.

I pull the door closed.

"Here. Get over here."

I step over to him and crouch down. He's got a bent Mountain Dew can in his hand. He pulls a baggie of what I'm betting is marijuana out of his shirt pocket and pinches a bit of it and sets it on the already charred pin-prick holes near the back of the can. "See, Wilkins, this is how we'll make it through this scorcher. I mean, Christ, Louie has got to want to fucking kill us, having us work outside today. Here," he says, sparking the Bic and pushing the can to me, "your turn."

"No," I say.

Justin hesitates, the flame still dancing at the top of the Bic. "What the fuck?" he says.

I don't say anything, just stand and push my way out of the shed. I stumble, blink in the light but quickly make my way toward the weed-eater. I feel stupid, my face even hotter than before. No one smokes marijuana around here. It's just not done. Out here you can get stone drunk, shoot out the streetlights, make it with the deputy's daughter, and still be forgiven—but you better stay far away from weed and pills and that kind of thing. A few summers ago, some boys a few years out of high school broke into the Snakepit and stole thousands of dollars' worth of booze and cash and lottery tickets. They got caught, they spent a year of weekends in the county jail, and they still drink at the Snakepit today. It's that easy, it's even expected. But those Mexicans, the ones logging the

Bull Mountains south of town—everyone claims they're selling marijuana and methamphetamine, and they might as well not exist for the way we pass by them in the café. I know it doesn't make any sense, but I'm furious that Justin has forced me to choose this place and its ridiculous rules—because I can't lose this job. I need it, to save for college. And I won't give up that dream, not even for the music.

I may not like the work, but I'll do it. Until she landed a full-time teaching job and leased out the ranch, my mother woke before the sun and slogged through miles of ditch water to set the irrigation—and then walked back to the house and cleaned up and drove to her day job. It was what she had to do to keep food on the table, to keep her three kids in school clothes and books and dreams of college. That's me, I think. I don't care how hot it is outside. I'll work. I'll earn it. Not like Justin—Justin taking too many cigarette breaks, Justin napping in the band room, Justin clowning around when he's supposed to be power-washing the buses, and then I have to power-wash the buses.

Yet as I pick up the weed-eater, the gasoline sloshing in the tank, I think that there is something at stake here beyond buses and rules and dreams. For if Louie caught us not only would I lose my job—but our summer of Winstons and driving back roads and Nirvana lyrics would just like that be over.

My heart thwocks in my chest, my arms fairly tremble. I feel like I might cry. I pull-start the weed-eater, fire the trigger, and the nylon cord bites into a thick stand of horseweed.

WE HAD been for weeks inseparable. And even now, years later, I can still feel the hot wash of anger rise in me, a twinge of that chest-tight drama that is everything when you're sixteen. In the days after I fled the supply shed I felt at moments as if my very friendship with Justin betrayed everything I was working for, everything I knew. But then, a minute later, it seemed I had failed some crucial test, proved myself incapable of seeing beyond this mean world. *Oh well, whatever, nevermind—.*

I stay sullen and sulky for a day or two, but soon it's just a pain in the ass. It's so easy to smile with Justin, to sing and smoke Winstons and goof around. Even Louie, who every morning still tells Justin to get his goddamn hair cut, likes how Justin kids around with him, lets Justin talk him into letting us off early or switching the radio over to KROX. Soon, when Justin pulls out his baggie of weed, I don't blink. In fact, Justin works harder when he's high. So, when Justin convinces Louie to start letting us have two hours at noon, I ask Justin if he wants to come home for lunch with me.

"Fuck yes," he says. "Let me at those big ham sandwiches you always have."

So, here's Justin—holes in his jeans, greasy hair in his eyes, a cigarette back of his ear—sitting at my mother's kitchen table. Here's Justin saying, "Thank you," saying, "Yes, ma'am," saying, "Boy, this lemonade is nice." Here's Justin looking out the window, saying, "It sure is beautiful out here," saying, "You have quite a view."

My brother, who I have been filling full of Cobain and Cornell as well, stares wide-eyed and awestruck at Justin, at this prodigal son of sorts from out of the Seattle wilderness and happy to wash up at the sink, slick back his hair, brush the locust wings from his sleeves. My mother brings us a big platter of ham-and-butter sandwiches, tall glasses of milk, garden cucumbers sliced into wedges and dusted with salt. She sits and talks with us. She smiles, has a sandwich herself. We are there, then, in this world inside a world, and we are full and happy, the warm prairie wind rocking our drafty farmhouse, the cottonwoods and willows along the river bending in the wind.

THEN, ONE morning, Justin is late to work.

When he finally shows, he tells us he had to hitch a ride and that's why. "Because," he says, "think about it—how many cars come by on Highway 12 in an hour? Maybe three? And how many will pick up a longhaired hitchhiker? Think about that, Louie."

But then Justin turns his head. Under his ball cap his face is a blue wash of bruise, his hair crusted with blood, ropey scabs ringing the back of his neck and shoulders. We stare and stare at him. "My uncle," he says, finally. "He got drunk this weekend and took a logging chain to me."

"What for?" we ask.

Justin shakes his head.

Louie stamps and rages. "Because he's no better than a nigger! Nothing but a nigger is what he is!" Carol tells Louie to shut up and takes Justin to the bathroom to clean him up.

And while Louis rages, while Carol scrubs the blood out of Justin's hair, I work the toe of my tennis shoe over the short, gray institutional carpeting. Sweep it one way, and it dulls in the fluorescent lights. The other way, it glisters. We are, suddenly, in this world again. I don't want to be in this old world. I know I should be thinking of Justin, but I am thinking of myself. I am sixteen and confused, sad for my friend and sad for me. *Who knows?* the sad man sang. *Not me. I never lost control. You're face to face with the man who sold the world.*

That afternoon Louie lets us work inside, in the air-conditioning; he has us sweeping the machine shop, little curlicues of sawdust and metal shavings wheeling across the stone floor. For a long time we sweep and sweep and talk about music and girls and everything but those fierce, bright bruises. Finally, I tell him he should get out of his uncle's house but stay in town. I tell him he can't leave. I tell him there are some folks around here who take in foster children. Once I say it,

I get excited about it. I think maybe it would work. "You can get into a foster home, and then things would be all right. Right?"

"Yeah," he says, leaning on his broom and thinking a moment. "But I've heard of some real shitty foster homes. I mean, it'd have to be the right foster home. Maybe someplace with someone like your mom. Yeah, that's what it would have to be!" Now Justin is the one who's excited, dropping his broom and talking and planning, and I understand—and it hurts, this understanding—that Justin has been wanting this whole time not the world we fashioned for ourselves, but this world, my world.

IT IS near midnight. We are out at the oil wells. We have two handles of cheap vodka, a case of Olympia Ice. With us are some other boys, but Justin and I are the drunkest, the loudest, the ones climbing up the iron stairs of the rig, crawling out onto the black iron of the well hammer, out to where it nods up and down in the night some hundreds of feet above the earth. Earlier, we talked to my mother. She thinks Justin can stay with us for a while, at least until school starts, but then he may want to find a more permanent home in Roundup or Billings. She says not to get our hopes up, that we'll have to see what happens. But what to do about hope? This night the stars are a wash of white fire across the sky. And here in the sky, atop the nodding hammer of the well, Justin is finally telling me stories, telling me that it was last winter—February, after they got kicked out of their apartment—that his mother left. Telling me about his uncle, how he knew about his uncle's drinking and stayed on his own in Seattle for as long as he could. Telling me he sold things, carried things from here to there. Telling me he smoked what there was to smoke, swallowed pills when there were pills, slept wherever he could. Telling me he was hungry, telling me he was hungry. He is the one telling stories, and I am the one listening—but these Seattle stories are of a world gone wrong, the way the man screams in his songs.

For a long time he tells me these stories, and for a long time we ride the black iron of the well hammer through the black night. We are nowhere but the sky. We are anything but what we are: two boys from two very different places, two boys hoping and dreaming and drunk, two boys climbing down out of the stars, wandering through the dark.

SCRAPING GUM from the undersides of the lunchroom tables, I lecture Justin about how it won't be easy to toe the line, stick to the straight and narrow, be the kind of foster son my mother will demand. I tell him about family dinners, and chores, and curfew, and homework, and hand-me-down jeans, and no slacking off or smoking in the supply shed when you're supposed to be working. Again, I am telling him how this world, even for the good roof we sleep under and my mother's ham-and-butter sandwiches, is still full of dust and dead fathers and mean-ass rednecks and a dozen radio stations all playing bad country music.

"I know," he says. "I know. I don't care. It's what I want."

"You don't know," I say, though that's not what I mean to say. There in the fluorescent lunchroom, wads of chipped gum littering the floor, I don't know what I mean to say. But now, nearly twenty years on, I think I have some idea: I mean to say, I'm scared. I'm scared that this world you think you want won't be enough. Justin, if you move in with us, if you become my brother, even when I leave I won't be able to leave. You'll have to leave, too. And leave carrying your own dreams. Justin, you have to live in the world. You have to believe what the world might be. You have to do both. You have to believe the stories. "You need to listen to me," I say.

"Listen?" he says, and brushes his hair back of his ears. "You don't know. You don't know a fucking thing. So your old man dies. So you live out the sticks. So what? You've got it fucking made, man. You and your stories—you think all that matters? No, this is real. This is my chance. You better believe I'm going to fucking take it."

THE NEXT week, Justin doesn't show up for work.

We wait. We paint the coach's office. We paint the locker rooms. We take a break and stand around and blow on bad coffee in too-small Styrofoam cups. Louie cusses him for skipping out. Carol is worried he got beat up again, is hurt bad and can't make it in. I don't know what to think. He was going to come home with me today. That was the plan. He wasn't supposed to tell his uncle or anyone— just come home with me after work, come home to stay.

But now he's not here, and he's not here, and after lunch, finally, one of his cousins shows up and says Justin's gone but he'll work instead if we need him. He says this, and when we don't say anything, he says it again. He's small and sort of weasel-faced. He can't be more than twelve or thirteen but has driven into town anyway. Once, weeks ago, I stopped by their trailer to pick Justin up. There was a cord of wood on a flatbed pickup, chain saws and parts of chain saws littering the drive, maybe five or six rib-skinny kids mewling and screaming, running around half-naked in the dirt yard. His mousy aunt sat on the front steps. She didn't say a thing when I pulled up. His uncle walked out of the garage and eyed me a moment, yelled, "Justin. Justin, get your ass out here."

Louie stares at the cousin. Louie shakes his head. "No, kid. There's no work for you. Where's Justin?"

"Gone," the cousin says.

"Gone where?"

"I don't know. He and daddy got in a fight or something, and when I woke up Justin was gone. Daddy said he put him on a bus."

"Jesus," Louie says.

WE TRY to find him, ask around, make some calls. Nothing comes of any of it. A few years later, from that same cousin, I hear something about Justin joining the Job Corps down in Arizona. And that's the last I ever hear. It doesn't seem like enough. I don't tell Louie or Carol, I don't tell my mother. And like so many that live place to place and job to job, whether in cities or out on the plains, one day Justin's uncle and his aunt and all those dirty-cheeked cousins are as well just gone. It was years later. I was nineteen or twenty and home for the summer from college. I drove by their trailer because it was on the way, because I could, because it was something I had often done in the weeks and months after Justin disappeared—and there was nothing there. No curtains or blinds back of the windows, no windows, the door open and swaying four feet above the ground, the wooden steps leading up to it gone. The place looked gutted. As if it had been scraped clean with a blade.

Yet of any of us who were part of this story, strange as it sounds, I imagine it is his uncle—or maybe his aunt or that cousin—who knows where Justin is now, knows who he is, cares a bit about the way he makes his way through the world. Louie has retired and has too many troubles of his own: His only brother crushed to death in a work accident, his mother wandering with Alzheimer's. Carol has divorced and moved to Miles City. And my mother is an old woman, living out on the plains in that same drafty farmhouse.

And I am thirty-three years old, a college professor, and I have moved far away from eastern Montana, moved through and into worlds I had only read about and imagined before, and somewhere along the line, maybe because I couldn't sing or play guitar, I started writing poems. One of the first I ever published carried the epigraph *for Justin*. I was lying. It was for me, they've all been for me. Sometimes, I think I see him sitting in the back of my classroom, his jeans unwashed, dirty hair in his eyes. Or he's that skinny boy already around the corner. Or that one, standing there on the street, his shoulders bird-like, angular. Sometimes he smiles his beatific, sloppy smile at the woman who sees him seeing her and clutches her purse that much more tightly to herself.

Then, sometimes, he is a woman, say that sky-eyed girl with the hood of her sweatshirt pulled tight around her face. She slumps on the sidewalk, smoking cigarette after cigarette. For a long time I watch her from across the street. Like I do when I am in the bookstore, and I see him out there wandering in the rain.

Sometimes when he is out there in the rain, I see that he is alone and down to his last smoke, that he is confused and hurt and hungry for ham-and-butter sandwiches.

Sometimes when he is out there I see something that was once there has died now in his eyes. Sometimes he comes in out of the rain and shakes his wet head and is too loud where he should not be loud.

Sometimes I am scared and turn away and wish he would leave.

Sometimes he does leave.

Sometimes I forget all about the music and him. But then, in East Des Moines, a winter highway, strip malls, a boy with a thin denim jacket wrapped around his frost-shattered ears: That's him, that's Justin—right there: And I see him, and he sees me, and I don't know about him, but here is never where I thought I would be.

A Fragment from
My Grandfather's Body

YOU READY?

I AM SIXTEEN and driving fast down Highway 12. My younger brother and Carlo, who stays with us when he's fighting with his brothers, are in the backseat taking pulls of cheap vodka straight from the bottle. Daisy Laird, dark-eyed and slender and beautiful as moonlight, is sitting next to me. Carlo hands me a beer. I pop the top and take a long swig. Daisy smiles and the stars go wild in the sky. I drop the pedal to the floor. We hurtle through engine grind and frog song, beer foam and brash laughter, and finally skid to a gravelly stop in front of our house. My mother is gone for the weekend, and though our grandparents live just a quarter mile down the road, my brother and I tell everyone not to worry: "Just keep it quiet," we say.

Then, for what seems like hours, there is only the smooth line of Daisy's shoulders, her hair falling across her face. But too soon she's gone, always careful to beat her father—still holding his stool to the sawdust floor of the Sportsman Bar—back home, and B.J. Murnion shows up with some girls from Roundup, three cases of beer, and a shotgun. Stars explode across the sky.

And then it's early in the morning, the sun just a rim of light in the east, and someone's knocking on something. Knocking hard. Rattling glass. I stumble out of bed and swing open the front door. The sun is low but already hot. My grandfather hands me a bucket of staples and a pair of fencing pliers. "You ready?" he asks. "There's fence to be walked up north."

All morning he idles behind me in the truck as I hammer staples and hold my aching head. By noon, I'm delirious. He lets me rest for a bit, then walks with me as we string wire and rip up rotten wood posts, the hot sun hanging heavy in the sky. My grandfather, even at eighty, walks the prairie fast and sure. I straggle behind.

SKINNY DREASE

"HE'LL HEAR," SHE says, her voice small and breathy.

"No," I say. "He won't."

And it's true. He's upstairs, one hand in the elastic waistband of his sweat pants, the other wrapped around a can of Keystone Light. He's watching whatever happens to be on television on a summer Saturday afternoon; he's always watching whatever happens to be on television. He is no longer Coach. Though all those years ago he tried and failed, at least he tried. Not anymore.

In all the time I have been dating his daughter he has said nothing at all of substance to me. So, now, he is just Skinny. Skinny because the Little League folded when I was ten; Skinny because my father is near ten years dead; Skinny because I am young and strong and think myself especially smart; Skinny because though not so old he is already a no-account, sweat-pants-wearing ghost haunting his own home—his wife at her beauty shop all hours of the day and his big red dual-cab pickup broke down in the front yard for the past three seasons. Most of all he is Skinny because when I bring his oldest daughter back stinking of beer and bonfire and river, I'd like him not to be already passed out on the couch. Just once I'd like him to rise up and get angry, send her to her room, say, big shouldered and stern, "Son, we need to talk."

"He won't," I say again, propping myself up on one elbow. And she looks at me with her wet, gray-green eyes and nods and swallows, then slips her T-shirt over her head.

JEFF THOMAS

MY BROTHER, CARLO, Jeff, and I are out at the oil wells smoking cigarettes and listening to Nirvana's *Unplugged* album after school—when up the road comes Rooster Crawford in his big pickup. Rooster drives right at us, as if he will not slow down, though, finally, he hits the breaks—the back tires biting into dirt and gravel, the whole pickup fishtailing to the left—and a wave of dust rises and breaks over us, small rocks pinging against our faces. Rooster graduated two years ago but is still hanging around, showing up at high school parties and spitting Copenhagen and giving titty-twisters. Rooster gets out now and slams the door behind him. He listens for a moment, then sneers. "What the fuck kind of faggoty music is this?"

Jeff, who the whole time has just been leaned back against the Tercel, taking it easy, snaps his cigarette to the ground. He looks at me, and we both straighten ourselves up and walk over to Rooster. Jeff is six feet, four inches tall, and he carries his 220 pounds in his chest and arms and thighs—his waist a slim thirty-two inches. Jeff and his older brother moved into town a few years ago, moved from a bigger town,

THE MOUNTAIN AND THE FATHERS

near the mountains. Like me, they are raised by their mother, and they are poor, and they don't cowboy but wear instead flannel shirts, baggy jeans, and Doc Martens, shaggy hair and sideburns—yet no one messes with the Thomas boys because they are both tremendous and tough and know exactly what they like and do not like. Though they listen to Justin's music, they don't slip around the edges and disappear: They are who they are; they walk with their big black boots right across the tops of things. And when Jeff's brother graduated and went off to college and left him on his own in our little cowboy town, Jeff had to pick someone. Over Tony and everyone, he picked me. Or he found me. Or I found him. Anyway, we are inseparable now. Friday nights, I stay at his house. There, we sneak out his second-story window and sit on the roof and look out over the sputtering lights of town and the shocking stretch of stars that cut the dark, and we smoke cigarettes and talk for hours about music and Jack Kerouac and how to get out of this impossibly small and small-minded town. We are going to go to the University of Montana, we decide, which is all the way across the state, in a liberal town in the mountains. We are going to read and study and maybe become journalists or artists or Buddhists. We are going to drive the whole coast from Seattle to Oregon to California, and on down to Mexico. We are not going to let our lives be dictated by this place.

When we are just a few steps from Rooster, Jeff says, calmly, "Get the fuck out of here. No one wants you around. Do you want him around, Joe?"

"No," I say, looking right at Rooster. "Not at all."

"See?" Jeff says, lightly, as if the problem has been solved. "What did I tell you? Now, do yourself a favor. Get the fuck out of here."

Rooster spits, looks from one of us to the other. Without a word, he gets back in his pickup and drives away. He drives away.

Jeff turns and grins and playfully slicks back his eyebrows, then pulls an imaginary six-shooter from an imaginary holster and fires, blows smoke from the barrel. We laugh, turn the music up.

But then, like Rooster and all the others, Jeff's older brother quits college. He does not work and lives in an apartment above a bar in that town they came from, which is really not that big, not all that much different than Melstone. Jeff takes me there one weekend. We park in the alley and climb through a close, fetid stairway. We crack the door, and light falls blue across our faces. No one greets us, so we wander in. A blank-eyed girl sits in the middle of the front room. She wears bell-bottom jeans and a black brassiere. In her lap she cradles a plastic bottle of vodka, which is almost as big around as she is. There is a silver ring through her nose. The men (or are they boys? I can't tell anymore) slouch about on ratty chairs and couches. Music riffs and bends around us. No one says anything to us. No one says anything. I know I should not act surprised—Jeff isn't acting surprised—but I am surprised. Though the setting and accessories are different, it feels just like any too-late, far-gone party in a trailer house. The girl rises now, ceremoniously, and turns herself around the room and finally takes the hand of a boy with patch, black heard.

Later that night, after we have left the apartment and gone to some abandoned house in the country, two boys pull their shirts off and slam each other into walls. Then everyone runs into the hills and hides from the cops. I lose Jeff. I can't find him, and I can't find him, and I end up sleeping in the backseat of my car. In the glaring, midday sun, I wake. I am bleary, hungover. I drive up and down Main Street looking for Jeff. I don't know where he is. I leave town without him.

Years later—after his brother's death, after he has left college—I find Jeff in a duplex in Billings. He looks good, as big and tough as ever, and he has a steady girlfriend, a decent job at the mall. He has quit drinking and smoking, his only vice now the Copenhagen bulging his lip. He looks as whole and happy as he did all those years ago when we traded stories and dreams leaning back on the roof of his house. I am glad for him. He says that he's glad I came by, that he has a lot to tell me. He spits and wipes his mouth with the back of his hand and says he sees now how far he strayed. He says the only answer is Christ, that it was blasphemy to think we could find our own way, blasphemy to think we can find answers in just any old book. Blasphemies our many dreams.

WAYNE MEREDITH

I HAVE BEEN crisscrossing the horse camp pasture on the four-wheeler for nearly six hours now, the dust of my passing a cloud around me as I roar up the sand rocks and down the piney coulees of the Bull Mountains. I am after toadflax and knapweed, those blossoming but noxious weeds that have taken root across this logging-scarred land.

It is mid-July, hell's own season here in eastern Montana, and though the chemicals that slosh through the tank strapped to the back of the four-wheeler are milky and deadly, I have peeled off my hat, gloves, and shirt. When I find a patch of toadflax, I take the wand from the back of the four-wheeler and begin to spray—always the wind twisting around the sand rocks, eddying in the coulees—and the poison falls cool and lovely across my sunburnt body.

This is the work I do for Wayne Meredith. This and fixing fence and cutting hay and driving the grain truck: work that's dangerous, muscle-hardening, mind-numbing—and all there is for a boy to do out here. The Meredith ranch is deep in the Bull Mountains, some thirty miles south of our place, so during the week I live in an old homesteader's shack out here in the hills and take my meals with Wayne and his wife, Rosella. I have done this—fixed these four-strand barbed-wire fences and trailed these ornery Angus bulls and sprayed this poison—for three summers now. I am eighteen years old. I know no other life.

Yet I wish mightily that I did. Soon, I will leave Montana, will go off to college—though I might as well be gone now. All day I drift and dream, always somewhere else in my head, maybe in the last book I read or some bright world of my own making—so far away I don't even notice the western sky going bruise black, the lightning-like ragged scars. A peal of thunder snaps me back. The first small hailstones begin to fall and ring on the rocks. Hail, but thank Christ for a little rain. Let it shake and pop all it wants—as long as there's rain enough to wet the dust, to cool my seething, poison-soaked skin.

When I get back in the evening, I tell Wayne how much ground I covered, how much spray I used. He nods, hooks his thumbs in his belt loops. I see the combine is in the shop, so I know that's what he's been working on this afternoon as the hail came down. Like some laconic western cliché, we stare for a moment at the buttes and hills off in the west, the red sun slipping slowly behind them. We don't ever have much to say to one another. I don't even know whether to call him "Wayne" or "Mr. Meredith." If I can help it, I don't say either. He's a good man. I can see that. He runs his ranch right, treats his wife well, pays more than most around here do. And he likes me, maybe once or twice a summer says, "Good job." But I guess I had this idea that we would work together, and Wayne would see what a hand I was, how hardworking and savvy, and slowly we would begin to talk, to—though these are words I would never use with him or anyone else around here—connect, form a relationship. But we seldom work together, and speak only when it is necessary. This evening, like most evenings, we walk silently down the dirt road to the main house, where dinner—I can smell it as soon as I step in the door—is meat lasagna. We unlace our boots and fold back the sleeves of our snap shirts and wash up and sit at the dining room table. Rosella serves us bowls of lettuce slathered in ranch dressing and plates heaped with cheese and noodles and meat. She brings Wayne a can of Coors, me a Mountain Dew, and we eat. Besides Rosella worrying over a burnt noodle or two, no one says a thing.

Later, after dinner, after I have changed shirts and washed my face, the poison's white stain still freckling my neck and shoulders, I drive south down Custer Road, drive too fast, twisting my old GMC pickup through the moonlit hills, over the iron bridge, and on into town. I know I must be up tomorrow with the sun. I know nothing's going on, save maybe a few boys kicking rocks down Main, a knot of girls smoking in front of the Sportsman Bar—but I feel if I don't hear someone speak, if I don't get out of my own head, if I don't say something, I just might explode.

OUT WEST, PART TWO

NOW YOU'RE THIRTEEN, old enough to hunt by yourself, so you load the bolt-action .22 with shells. You walk north. There is little wind, the sun a white hole in the sky. Beneath your boots the bones of dry grass bend and crack. You feel good about this. Prairie dogs are bad for the fields. They spread disease. A sheep will snap a front leg in a dog hole. Your father is dead, your grandfather is old, and you tell yourself you are just doing what a man does. You are taking care of the fields, keeping the stock safe.

You tell yourself all kinds of things.

In the middle of the field, over a gray pile of culled fence posts, you lay your skinny body down. The prairie dogs—fat, round little rodents the size of a big rat or rabbit, their stub tails wagging with every chirp and bark—run and dash and scamper to their mounds, now stand and yip at one another. You close your left eye and snug the rifle butt up against your shoulder, the polished wood cool and smooth on the warm skin of your cheek. There's a fat one not fifty yards away. You steady yourself. There is the smell of creosote, the taste of dust and rank weeds. You sight along the blue barrel and pull

157

the trigger. There is a small pop. The prairie dog flops over and rolls down its mound and is dead.

You are pleased with yourself. You stand for a better look. From beneath the rotten posts, a cottontail rabbit zigzags out some twenty feet and stops, sniffs, and twitches its ears. You step back with your right foot and swing the rifle up to your shoulder again.

There's no need to shoot rabbits. You close your left eye. You don't eat rabbits; rabbits don't do any damage to the fields. You drop the open sights over the rabbit's spine. Its long ears twitch one, two, three times. You squeeze the trigger.

The rabbit bucks and jumps, screams.

You didn't know rabbits could scream. You shoot again. And again. It's still screaming, back legs kicking at the empty air. You shoot again. The body bucks and jumps and is still.

Your breath comes back to you. That wasn't so bad, you think—but you won't tell your grandfather. He wouldn't like you killing rabbits. There's no sustenance to be had here; there's no beauty in shooting a still rabbit at twenty feet; there's nothing in this hunt but the killing. Your grandfather wouldn't have it.

He's old, though, and what does he know? Who really cares about rabbits anyway? All the older boys you run around with at school shoot them.

IT'S SATURDAY night. You are fourteen, nearly grown, you think—your grandfather older and older yet, his once board-straight shoulders beginning to buckle and slump, and your mother still tired, voiceless, and sad-eyed as you slam the screen door and screech the truck's tires on your way out.

You drive on into Melstone and park down by the Sportsman Bar. You get in with that bunch of older boys. They've got cigarettes, beer in the backseat, a bottle of whiskey they're passing around. Boy, they drive fast. They take the corners at a gravelly skid and raise dust right through the middle of town. Now, they race on out to the river, where you all pile out and run and yell and knock down the sign that says Primitive Road, the one that says Narrow Bridge. Someone starts throwing beer bottles at the old homesteader's shack off in the willows. They crash and shatter, the glass lovely in the light of the moon. One boy runs up on the bridge and strips off his clothes and jumps. Everyone cheers and yells. From somewhere down in the watery dark, he yells back.

You don't like this. You know this isn't any good. You're all drunk. It's dark. The water's fast and cold this spring. And who knows how deep it is here, anyway? Doesn't anyone remember the Morgan boy? You've seen him, slouched in his wheelchair, sucking can after can of 7-Up through a straw.

But all of a sudden—you don't quite know how it happens—you're there with the other boys, in line, laughing right there behind them. Each jumps in turn, and now it's your turn: You don't know what to do about this. The other boys cheer and holler. Someone passes you the whiskey bottle. You take a big swig, wing off your T-shirt, edge your toes over the rusted iron—into the dark, you leap.

AND FOR a good while, that's how it goes:

We drive fast and wild out into the dark, coax girls down to river-bottom bonfire parties, stand on the beer cooler in the back of Tony's truck and flood the dark trees with a spotlight—Chip shoots and hits the coon between the eyes, hollers, sprays beer foam everywhere.

But then, late one night on my way back from Addie Mae's trailer, where I smoked Winstons and drank Bud Ice and laughed along like I knew what I was doing, I come over Hougen's Hill out of Melstone headed west at about ninety miles an hour right down the middle of the road. My headlights shift from sky to highway, and there, straddling the double yellow line, is a big Angus. I'm in the old Tercel; that cow's as big as this car. I spin the wheel this way and that way—and the night spins around me.

Strangely, I'm not scared.

A little angry, maybe. But as the stars arc and wheel over the wheeling hills, it is like a thing coming down that I knew would always come down, the way I know my old grandfather will only grow older and that skinny sophomore I like will take up with some twenty-seven-year-old ranch hand and Chip will end up knocking over the liquor store in Roundup. There is nothing to do now but let go. There goes basketball, I think. There goes just about everything.

And then everything is still.

And I am in the middle of the road, facing east instead of west, headlights veering off into the dark. I turn the car around and drive slowly toward home, make it nearly to our turnoff before the shaking starts.

I fall into bed with my jeans on, my arms and shoulders and face and heart jerking, banging like a screen door slapped about in the wind. My dark breath runs from me like water.

I don't sleep until I see the sun.

Then, I dream.

Then, miraculously, I wake.

TEN-ODD YEARS later the night is dark and shot with stars, the red tracers of lit cigarettes, a scattered rainbow of light from the dance hall.

It's a cover band, mostly George Strait numbers, some old Eric Clapton. And this is the All-School Reunion. Melstone is so small there are no individual class reunions; instead, every ten years or so, anyone who ever graduated from the local high school shows up for two days of handshakes and hellos, Main Street bonfires, beer gardens, and big stories. So that's where I am, at the All School Reunion, sipping a beer and leaning up against someone's pickup. It's very late. My wife, Liz, has been asking to leave. And we should. But maybe just one more beer. A friend of mine from college, who didn't graduate from Melstone but happened to be passing through Montana when we were passing through Montana, has had even more to drink than I have. He's telling me something—something sad, I think—but I'm not really listening. I'm staring at the stars.

Now two older men are in front of my friend and me. I try to concentrate on them. One is Kevin Kincheloe. I know him. He's a good guy. I used to play with his oldest daughter, Janna, during the noon recess up at school. She was small and dark-haired, and I thought she was beautiful. But when I was in the third grade, just after my father died, they had to move away. The bank foreclosed. They lost their ranch and everything else. I think Kevin works some kind of wage job up around Billings now.

Anyway, Kevin says hello, shakes my hand, offers us a pull off his fifth of Southern Comfort and starts telling some story. But now the other man shoulders his way up to us. He's big and fat, his face wide and whiskered. His shirt is untucked, the snaps undone nearly to his belly. Kevin starts to introduce him, but the fat man cuts him off and says something stupid. My friend says something stupid back. The fat man thumps my friend in the chest with his meaty finger—and the air around us goes glass.

Kevin slides back half a step and quits talking, his mouth dropping into a hard line. This man is a father of two daughters, I think, surprised to find Kevin readying himself, to find that I too am straightening up, my arms loose, my hands curling into fists at my sides. My friend, stepping toward the fat man, sneering at the fat man, slowly raises the bottle of Southern Comfort and takes a long drink. Then he takes another. He wipes his mouth with the back of his hand, shoves the bottle hard into the fat man's chest, says, "I want to see *you* drink."

The fat man stands there for a moment. Then drinks—one, two, three, four swallows. My friend, still rigid and pissed and sneering at the fat man, nods with each swallow. The fat man lowers the bottle and hands it to Kevin, who drinks, and then hands the bottle to me. So I drink, the syrupy bourbon coating my throat—and somehow, for no decent reason at all, this solves the whole mess: The fat man belches and turns away; my friend laughs and stumbles a bit, sits on his ass in the gravel; I breathe and let my shoulders go soft; Kevin smiles drunkenly and steps toward me and starts in again on what-ever story he was telling in the first place.

I lean back up against the hard, cool steel of the truck to watch the stars open and close their bright and tiny mouths. I am surprised at myself. Here I am: a college professor going soft in the middle think-ing I'm going to get into a fistfight. I've never been in a fistfight. Even when I was an idiot-hearted boy, drinking too much and driving too fast and doing stupid things out there in the night, I always stopped before I stepped into that kind of violence. I always turned away. I saw it all right, I even rushed in and grabbed a boy or a man and broke up a fistfight or three—but I never threw a punch myself. What would I have done tonight? What would Kevin have done? What might have happened?

I'm still idiot-hearted, I think, and then try very hard to quit thinking. Kevin's saying something now about how much he misses the people out here, the Sportsman Bar, the good land along the river they used to own.

THE LAND out on the Big Dry was bad, but we tried hard to make it good:

We drained the river for irrigation, we tore out the cottonwoods and plowed up the river bottom, we set out tubs of used motor oil for grasshopper traps. We sprayed the fields for knapweed and fox-tail, we fertilized and irrigated and sprayed for weeds. We stayed all night in the shed to pull breech lambs, we wormed and vaccinated and dehorned, we fed tons and tons of corn. And when none of it worked, when the wheat still burned and the grasshoppers descended like the seventh sign of Revelation and the sheep went bone skinny in the sun, when that bad land still beat us, we prayed. And when that didn't work, we cursed. And then we slung the bodies to the boneyard and tried again—harder this time, the wheels greased with another layer of our bile.

Even done well, you couldn't call it a living; it was all a kind of ritualized dying. And that's not to demean a way of life. It's simply to call it like it is. Living off the land, any land, is hard. Living off that bad land, part of the stretch of high plains along the eastern front of the Rockies they used to call the Great American Desert, was nearly impossible. Especially when the rules of agriculture changed under Nixon and Reagan, when we went from raising sheep and cattle and chickens and hay and wheat and oats and a little of just about every-thing else to cattle and corn and that's it, which was about the same time the summers got longer and the winters shorter and the spring creeks that once ran in all the coulees just dried up. And even then we didn't do anything different. We didn't advocate for ourselves or educate ourselves. We just doubled down and got tougher, worked harder—more loans from the bank, more acres grazed to the ground, more chemicals washed across the land.

We hurt the land, and it hurt us. Sometimes it hurt us physically: I didn't know a man in the valley who wasn't missing a couple of fingers, or maybe recovering from a broken leg after being thrown, again, by that ornery mare. There were boys in wheelchairs, girls with barbed-wire scars down their faces. Women who were forty looked sixty-five, and women who were sixty-five looked downright biblical. Clyde Brewer's heart blew up. Multiple sclerosis took hold of Butch Treible's straight spine and shook it crooked. And when I was nine, my father turned to the wall and died of cancer, probably exacerbated, they told us, by prolonged exposure to potent herbicides.

And sometimes it struck not us, but what we loved: After my father died, my grandfather, who was one of the last of the old-time cowboys to ride the Comanche Flats before barbed wire, who deeply knew and dearly loved this land, sold the family ranch. And then he told us boys a new story: He told us we would leave this place and go off to college. He only had an eighth-grade education, but that's the story he started telling, all about the things we could do if we only buckled down and kept at those books. It was a good story; it was the same story my mother was telling us. You see, so many of the other stories weren't working anymore, those ones other men told to their sons and grandsons, the ones about that good land along the river, about how some great-grandfather settled it way back when, about how it was hard going but they made it, about how even in the worst of times the land would see them through, about how the land was theirs and had been theirs and would always be theirs. But then when their boys got ready to start working that land, turned to that land— it was gone. Where'd it go?

Ask the Crow, the Northern Cheyenne, the Sioux. Out west, all the old mistakes are new, and many men, good men like Kevin Kincheloe, had to sit at their kitchen tables and watch through the front window as the bank's auctioneer walked their acres, selling everything, from combines to skinny cattle—selling it all right down to the dry grass. Imagine it for a moment: Everything you love of the world taken from you. Now imagine it being taken from your child.

It was all about the land. We didn't do right by it, and we lost it. The phone rings, and my mother shakes her head, adds another name to the list of farm foreclosures. The neighbors, the few left, sit silently at the kitchen table, the clink of coffee cups saying all there is to say. It was a slow, psychic violence. And many turned that violence inward. Over another shot of Rich & Rare at some hole of a roadside bar, men hatched a thousand plots for revenge. Boys closed their blue eyes and drove hell-bent down gravel roads. Women left screen doors screeching on their hinges. Girls climbed in with whoever had a fast car headed somewhere else.

That's mostly what folks did: They left. And they left like leaving was some kind of answer, like you're not carrying your bad heart out into the hot night, loading into the one pickup the boss won't miss that much a saddle and some tack and that vodka box the kids packed lip-full of toys, and driving too fast then through the star-shot dark, trying decide on either Harlowton or Big Timber, or maybe up and do it and make for Kalispell. On the television, politicians talked about this program or that program to help rural America, but some-one knew what it was really all about—they set up a suicide hotline strictly for farmers and ranchers who'd gone bankrupt and had to sell, who found themselves stuck in a world they didn't recognize.

But, too, there were those who picked up their rifles and, instead of slipping the barrel under their own chins, shouldered them, drew a bead on the world. Like that bunch in Jordan, Montana, calling themselves the Freemen, barricading themselves in a place they dubbed Justus Township. They held off the feds for weeks with a big arsenal and bigger threats. The press called them a militia group, a onetime thing, a bunch of crazies—but they were just ranchers who had lost their land, folks like so many who had fallen into reactionary politics. Others got fundamental, went back to church in a big way, started thinking the books in the library or the new schoolteacher's ideas were to blame. And some just struck out at whoever or what-ever happened to be in the way.

It was historical: smallpox blankets, slaughtered buffalo, and plowed prairie grass gave our ancestors the land in the first place. Maybe more blood could get it back.

I WAS just sixteen the first time I saw a person try to kill another person.

I had parked at the café and was riding around with some older boys in a pickup. One of them had just been dumped by his girlfriend and he was angry, really angry—swearing and pounding the window with his fist and telling us again and again what he ought to do, what he would do. When he spotted her car pulling onto Main Street, he yelled at the boy driving to follow her. *Follow her!*

So we did. We tailed her through town. We yelled when we got close, swore and said all kinds of things. And when she took off down the highway, we came after her. We cranked it up to a hundred and pulled even with her and threw pop cans at her windshield. We followed her when she turned off onto a gravel road, when she turned off into a field of sagebrush, when she skidded to a dusty stop in the middle of nowhere. I was scared, but I piled out of the pickup like the other boys, ready to yell, ready to stomp around and act mad, ready to do something. And when that girl threw open her car door and shouldered a rifle and started shooting, like the other boys I took off across the prairie.

She was yelling and crying, shaking something terrible. Her father, I knew, was a bad drunk. He'd sold off, leased, or lost most of their land and a few months back left the family for a cocktail waitress and an abandoned trailer house. I'd still see him sometimes, at ball games or in the café. He'd stumble over to me and shake my hand and try to tell me funny stories about my father, though he couldn't ever remember how they ended and always got them twisted up. Anyway, she must have shot five or six times, maybe more. After a moment,

166

the last report still clanging along the hills, she dropped the rifle and collapsed there beside it in the dust.

We all ran back to the pickup and got in and drove away.

CAN YOU imagine? I thought I could just up and leave it all behind. I thought, as I left for college a few years later, I was getting clean away.

But when I start graduate school, instead of renting an apartment in town, we settle in a little white house down the highway near the crossroads of Bovill, Idaho. Out our backdoor the Bitterroot Mountains rise up with their blue faces of cedar and pine. In the mornings, I run along the creek down to the log works, the smell of stone and water and sweet sap strong in the air. Liz brings home buckets of blackberries from the canyon. We make pancakes for dinner, cover them with berries and cream. We've been traveling for a few years, living here and there, and are happy to be back in the West—this place we feel we know, this wide open we both love.

Saturday night, we head over to the Elk Bar. It's a one-room joint in the ground floor of the old Bovill Hotel, a pile of bricks that looks like it might collapse if you kicked it hard enough. I order two bottles of High Life and two shots of Jim Beam. We smile at one another, say, "Here's to the West!" Then clink our shot glasses and drink, seal our toast with a whiskey kiss. We take our beers and wander over to the jukebox and lean down to read the yellowing song titles. I pick a Hank Williams tune. Liz goes for Patsy Cline. I start to say something to her—but suddenly she turns and yells.

There are two men: shirtless, stains on their faces, one leaning on a pool cue, the other working a wad of snoose around his mouth. They seem built out of wires and rough-cut boards, their stringy legs and thick chests and hands. Liz is yelling at them, stepping forward, pointing, her voice high and loud, her face hot. These men are half grinning, half pleading—saying they didn't know who she was, thought she was a girlfriend, a cousin. And suddenly, as the one with the snoose streak on his chin glances at me and wipes at his mouth, I get it. One of them has felt her up, grabbed her ass or something as we were bent over the jukebox. I feel my whole body go tight and ready. I step forward, in front of Liz, and say, "Leave my wife the fuck alone."

They grin at one another. They step forward too, their shoulders rolling back. The one wraps both hands around his pool stick. "Hey, man, I thought she was my girlfriend. She looks like my girlfriend. Honest mistake, right? No trouble, right? You don't want any trouble, do you?" It's a legitimate question. Because they do. They've forgotten Liz entirely. They're both staring right at me, the sweat shining on their bare chests, the stains, I see now, are blood bright on their faces. This is what they came for, this is what they wanted all along. And the rest of the bar knows this, too. They have quieted, hunkered down, turned ever so slightly our way. They're waiting, wondering. What will this man do, this skinny man who drives to the university each morning, this man we don't know, this outsider? Will he do the right thing? Will he swing? He ought to swing. That's his wife there. He ought to bust that beer bottle right across that boy's face. He'll get the shit kicked out of him then. Those boys are twice as mean as he is. You can see that plain as day. But that doesn't matter. He ought to swing.

I don't swing. I say, again, "Leave my wife the fuck alone," and I take her arm, and we leave. We walk down the street to the other bar in town, Bailey's, where I drink shot after shot of bourbon, where someone follows us from the Elk and tells us that it's a good thing we left because those boys just got laid off by the local logging company and have been strung out on meth for days and getting meaner each hour. But neither booze nor commiseration helps. I'm in a bad way. I'm in a darkness I haven't ever known. This is as close as I've ever been to fighting, and I'm furious that I didn't—furious that in that moment they could have done whatever they wanted, taken what I love most.

Later, as Liz sleeps, I go to the shed behind the house and stand in front of the rough-cut boards of the back wall. I swing and swing and my fists crack against the wood and soon the skin of my knuckles is shredded, my fingers swollen and bleeding. I beat the boards with my open hands, my elbows, my chest, my face.

I fall to my knees.

I breathe.

I stand and walk back into the house with my broken hands.

GO OVER it again: how it begins with the whims of wind and want, or maybe just some quick moment of stupidity; how failure and shame, even in an instant, become so impossibly heavy, a sack of stones you must shoulder; how this then is fear; and how fear someday detonates you—the slow implosion, the breakneck explosion.

But it doesn't have to be this way. We will fail, we will still act without good reason, we will always be burdened with failure and shame—but that, I think, is where things can change: There is a kind of awful and ready reverence that is some kin to fear but is not fear. It is when we understand the blood drying on our hands, the package of hand-wrapped meat we pull from the freezer. It is when we allow the usual beauty of our days, when we make reverent the work of sustenance. It is when we understand that we do not need to own the land to be of the land, when we admit that we all live on the land and take responsibility for what violence we do by our very lives unto the land. It is when we recognize how stories fail us and how stories save us. It is when we have heard them both and tell, in the moment of our greatest need, the story that will save us.

Like my grandfather. He knew and loved the way it had been, he saw the way it had to be. And always, even in the darkest of my days, my blood remembers his voice. I am here and mostly whole because of the stories he told me. We need to remember how it really was and is out west. And we need to tell those true, new stories.

Two Fragments from
My Grandfather's Body

BLUE, TO FURTHER BLUE

MY GRANDFATHER AND I are driving through the Bull Mountains up to the Klein Creek Mine for a load of furnace coal—and this time I am telling him stories. He listens, proud of all the things I've done in my two years at college. I keep talking, ramble about theology class and final exams and our project in computer science, though at just twenty years old—sure I know somewhere around ninety-five percent of everything there is to know and convinced I'll pick up the other five soon—I don't quite understand that he is humoring me. He nods and chews a toothpick, his right arm hooked out the open window of the pickup, wind on the flesh of his eighty-four-year-old face.

At the mine, we buy two tons of greasy coal from a man whose skin is smeared with soot. On the drive home, my grandfather wants to buy me a burger at the A&W in Roundup. In my zeal for social, environmental, and just about every other kind of justice out there, I've quit eating fast food—but I'm hungry and don't want to hurt his feelings, so I order a bacon cheeseburger, large fries, and a root beer float.

THE MOUNTAIN AND THE FATHERS

We pull up to the stone coal cellar in his yard. He backs the truck in, and we get out and grab big scoop shovels. I peel off my shirt and with a gravelly crunch sink the shovel into the black hunks. We shovel and shovel, and soon he tires. Then, my grandmother is there, wagging her finger, telling him to take it easy. She lectures him about what his doctor said and, finally, orders him down from the pickup bed. My grandfather is ashamed, but he listens to his wife of sixty years. I watch him walk to the house, the familiar hitch in his step, a new bend to his once board-straight shoulders.

I don't think much of it. My world of shining ideas and college girls, the world I scrambled into off the labor of his back, is so dazzling that I fail to see the dim edges of the horizon near the sagebrush hills where the light goes from blue, to further blue, to black. I have forgotten about Indian burns and broken bones and Uncle Okie. I have no idea what has happened to that old deck of poker cards. I haven't walked even a mile of fence since I left home. I sling another shovel full of coal to the cellar and wipe the sweat from my forehead.

DUST, JESUS, AND THE WIND

THE MUSK of wet oak and wine fills the shed as I pull the bung from a barrel of Wahluke Slope sangiovese, plunge the thief into the wine, and pull out half a liter. I do acid tests and yeast starters for a small winery along the Spokane River in the mornings, then, in the afternoon, sit around with the wine maker—talking, tasting, new wine wild on my tongue. I ride my bike back into the city after work, follow the river past the falls, my head fuzzy in the haze of summer afternoon. I have grown my hair long. I read William Carlos Williams and Theodore Roethke for hours. My roommate and I sit on the sagging porch of our college house and chain-smoke cigarettes. He's always talking about Dostoevsky, and I tell him all my grandfather's stories. I've fallen in love with a dark-haired girl. She's gorgeous and listens to Willie Nelson. On campus the dogwoods are furious with blossoms. At twenty-three, the world is new wine, and I am drinking, drinking.

Then my mother calls. The cancer's back.

It's in my grandfather's throat and wrapped black around his lungs. I ask her what hospital he's in, and she says they're keeping him at home, on the old leather sofa in the front room. "We can care for him best," she says, "here at home. It's only a matter of time."

But God, what time. Days later my mother calls again, crying down the distance. He's delirious, cursing dust, Jesus, and the wind. Hung flesh. Shit on towels. The stink of chaffing skin. White thighs and penis. His once strong body now a ruin.

And the pain. His screams are infantile, then animal, his bones given wholly to the deep rack and howl. But my mother says his hands still flutter to the sky. Sun dark and violent in his last strength, my grandfather's hands move with the rapture of work: Now he's stretching fence, swinging out his lariat, pulling, gently pulling, the new lamb from the emptiness of air. Then he grabs my mother's wrist, looks her in the eyes with wounded recognition, says, "Swede, it hurts. Swede, I'm dying here. Can't you help me?"

The taste of wine like ashes on my tongue. This is grief, I recognize the hollow ache of it from before, but this time death and grief make sense, and I give myself to sadness, scatter books across the floor, read my poets for their beautiful lies. I lie in bed, streetlights at my window, and try to dream my grandfather's stories.

Then I'm home—and the smell of sage is strong in the spring air. My brother and I wake at dawn and drive out onto the Big Dry. We stop in a swirl of dust and walk into the wind and sun, stare into the sloping distances. My mother once told us that Jim Maxwell's heaven was just a little north and west of Willow Creek, and we know this is holy ground. We can feel it with each step, our footfalls on the prairie earth as quiet and sure as his once were. We pluck fence wire and wrap our fingers around pine posts—our hands, which were for so long his, now wholly our own. We say very little. We both know he has given everything over to us—dark hands and breath and bones. We leave this swath of prairie for a final time and drive home.

This time, I remember everything:

The light falls mute and red through the stained and sainted glass. The wooden struts of the church arch up and over us. This priest never knew my grandfather, so Buster Knapp's son Roger, dressed in his best snap shirt and jeans, says the eulogy. Once we wheel him out, the funeral director tries to shut the casket, but my grandmother won't let him. She touches his face, holds his still shoulders one last time.

Then there is the slow procession up the high hill east of town, to the cemetery that looks out over the river's bend and the whole wide expanse of the Big Dry. Here, near dusk, along with my brother and my cousins—his grandsons, now nearly all grown into men—I carry my grandfather over bunchgrass and pear cactus to the crest of the hill. I weep and stumble. How good it is to weep and understand. Here, the wind stings my wet, raw face. Here, the grass cracks beneath my steps. This is as it ought to be: the wind ripping at the land, my grandfather heavy in my hands. The old grow old and die. The young grow old and grieve. I owe him for this one last lesson. Already he has taught me living. Now he teaches me to die. Dust rises from our steps. Lightly, we set his broken body in the ground.

V.

The feelings of that night

were so near . . . I could reach out

and touch them with my hand.

I had the sense

of coming home to myself.

—WILLA CATHER

THE BIG DRY

IT WAS SOME years ago now when I last talked with Carlo Bernard. He called late on a Sunday evening, told me he'd called my mother and got my number. He was ranch-sitting in the foothills of the Snowy Mountains. I was finishing grad school at the University of Idaho. He'd just bought a '97 Toyota pickup with a rebuilt engine. I'd gotten married a few years ago. He hadn't seen Tony or Chip or any of the old crew in years. Neither had I. He told me he was doing well—going to church, not drinking so much. He told me he might even go back to school. I was happy to hear it. He said next time I was home (as if Montana would always be home) to give him a ring. I said sure, then goodbye.

I sat, a little stunned, and tried to remember the last time I had seen Carlo. It must have been nearly five years before, at an old cowboy bar called the Jersey Lily. I could almost see him there: hand wrapped around a long neck bottle, wide grin on his face, and holes in his too-small jeans. My wife asked about the call, and I told her it was an old friend, Carlo, that I might have told her some stories about him. She nodded and asked how he was. I told her he seemed good, that he sounded good—but silently I was wondering if what he told me was

177

the truth, if he really was living in some pinewood lodge, if his truck even ran, if maybe he wasn't drinking at some tin-roofed roadside saloon most every night.

Carlo is big, or was when I knew him, and back then he always kept his head shaved. A raised and ragged scar ran across the side of his scalp, just over his left ear (though no one ever believed him, he often told us he'd fallen into the tire path of a stock truck that bumped right over his eight-year-old head). Carlo's eyes were green and gleaming, his face broad, and he had a bluish mark he said was some kind of burn brushed across his left cheek. His legs were thick, and to say his chest was barreled is an understatement: Double-barreled was more like it. His chest was so wide and strapped with muscle that he had to carry his arms out from his body, palms turned forward. He'd greet you—all down the length of the hallway at school or clear across a smoky barroom—by smiling and lifting his muscled arms to the sky.

CARLO'S FAMILY moved to Melstone, into the old Williamson place over near the Congregational Church, when I was ten. Though my family was Catholic and poor, we were more or less accepted by the local aristocracy—a handful of protestant ranching families, most of whom could trace their family line back to some of the first cattle ranchers and homesteaders in that part of the country, most of whom had been blessed as well with enough oil under the swales of their grazing land to buy brand new Ford pickups every spring.

It was my grandfather and my father who ensured this acceptance. Though my grandfather didn't buy his ranch until after the war and for that was always somewhat set apart from the other wide-bellied, grinning old patriarchs—he nonetheless impressed everyone he met as one hell of a cowboy and one hell of a hard worker. And before he died, my father, even though he was raised on a tobacco farm in

North Carolina and got bucked off every horse he ever tried to ride, had done the same with his Southern manners and talent for telling stories down at the Sportsman Bar. When Art Kincheloe loaned my young mother the money to finish her last semester of college, he told her it was because she was Jim Maxwell's daughter. And every time I walk into the Sportsman some red-faced rancher or another always offers to buy me a beer and starts in on what a fine man and good farmer Walt Wilkins was.

The Bernard boys, however, were a different story. There were four of them, all broad-faced and stout, and their old man sat on the porch day after day and growled through the smoke of his cigarettes. Mr. Bernard was immense and impressive—with his steak-thick hands and his voice booming up and out his wide gash of a mouth—but somehow not right, like the great ragged stump of a lightning-struck oak. And he took government checks for disability.

In our part of the country, disability or welfare was anathema: Any kind of assistance check branded you ignorant and weak, an easy victim of the Big Dry. The progression was plain: First you lost your land, then you took assistance, then you moved away, or died. Out on the far prairie, bad luck and bad choices were one and the same, failure the only unforgivable sin, for we had to believe we could abide in that bad land. We had to believe that it was possible, that it was not folly. Everything was at stake: the dignity of those who'd come before us, the dreams of those who came behind us, and, always, the substance of our every breathing day. So, we told the stories that made it so, stories of hardy homesteaders busting up sod in the oven of August and sticking it out even when the dust started to blow, stories of grizzled, won't-quit cowboys riding through cattle-high drifts of snow. We let the weak lambs die in birth-wet straw and slung their bodies in bloody piles by the shed gate, we laughed at clean jeans and city slickers and neon rodeo wannabes, we believed we were born meaner, stronger, and smarter, that the land itself had chosen us. And so we turned our backs on failure of all kinds, blamed it not on the undertaking, not on the variables of wind and want, but on the character of the participants. Though my widowed mother's part-time teacher's salary qualified us for food stamps and free lunch at school, she never took either. She was college-educated, outspoken at school board meetings, one of the few Democrats in the county, and in real danger of losing the family farm—but she knew taking assistance would have crossed the line.

Though the real damage was done by those disability checks, Carlo's mother didn't help matters any. She got right next to you when she talked, leaned in until her very breath was on your neck. She wore polyester pantsuits and dyed her hair a startling orange-red. She'd park herself on a stool in front of the poker machine down at the Snakepit and, when she started losing, say things like "Hell" and "Cocksucker" and "Well, fuck me up the ass running backwards." She tried to start a pornographic video shop in the old corner market, but the Congregational Church ladies got wind of it and all hell broke loose. And once, bringing Carlo home after a weekend spent pouring cheap vodka down our throats and chasing cowgirls over in Harlowton, Carlo's mother leaned into the porch rail, pulled hard on her menthol, and told my brother and me, "You boys are good for him, you know. You're just what he needs—some role models. He loves you goddamn boys."

I have no idea what disability Mr. Bernard suffered. He was an old man when he came to town, and Carlo told me he had fought in Korea and worked on oil wells all across the country and fathered other children with other women. And though I heard rumors—of sexual abuse as a child, of a violent former boyfriend—I also have no idea what memories haunted Mrs. Bernard. What I do know is that Mr. and Mrs. Bernard moved their brood of boys into the Williamson place, and then a double-wide down the street, and finally a prefab house some roustabout abandoned, and everyone in town, and everyone on the playground, decided right away that they weren't right, that they were dirty and poor and no good.

And from my perch near the teeter-totters, the Bernard boys did seem odd. They looked made of rocks and weeds, rusty nails. They swore and spit. They grinned through missing teeth. When the teacher wasn't looking, they struck wooden matches on their stone-washed jeans and tossed them to the gravel. The town kids often told me how after school the Bernard boys would chase cats up alleys and knock jackrabbits senseless with rocks, how they were suspected of stealing pop and candy bars at the Lazy JC. So I watched them carefully, I saw how different they were from Tony and Chip and the other boys, and I took note of my own crooked teeth and tousled hair. I was uncoordinated and dreamy and spent more time in the library than most of the girls, but even I could tell the Bernard boys were different enough to make me look like just another wolf in the pack.

TO BE honest about it, his name isn't even Carlo. It's Michael. At first, we all called him Mike or, because of the way his ears stuck out from his shaved head, Michael Mouse. We teased all the Bernard boys, but Michael definitely got it the worst. His older brother, Doug, had flunked two grades and, with his sleeveless jean jacket and homemade tattoos, was even bigger than most of the high schoolers. Though we tried making fun of him, after he punched D.J. Synoground in the mouth, we seldom did it to his face. The two younger boys, Henry and Luke, were small and always sick with something or other and had to get their pills each day from the school secretary. We decided it wouldn't be sporting. Michael, however, was just right. He was in the fourth grade when they first moved into town, one grade below me, and still the same size as the rest of us.

And Michael just attracted attention. He told such wild stories. He swore that his grandfather's surname had been Butcher and that he'd had to change it to Bernard after robbing a string of banks on horseback down in Arizona. He claimed to live summers out north on the McDaniel place. He let us all know that one of his cousins had been eaten by pigs and frequently detailed his many exploits with a girl named Peaches, who lived hours away and don't even try to find her. His stories twisted and turned on themselves; he often got lost in character or place and merged old stories with new, heightening the conflicts and changing the endings. Sometimes he fell off the back of the stock truck out north and his father drove right over his head, but then a few weeks later it would be his older half-brother carrying a load of hay somewhere near Billings.

Michael always had something in his pocket as well: an old knife, some rusty fishing lures, ivory dice. He'd dole out packs of his father's cigarettes to any of us boys who asked and steal his mother's trashy romance books so we could read the good parts behind the back wall at recess. But more often than not, once the fascination wore thin, we turned on Michael for these acts that he must have thought were a type of kindness: He was a liar, a thief, a pervert, too old for his age— just plain weird. He didn't do things like he should and neither did his parents, and we took it all as evidence that he somehow deserved the secondhand clothes he wore and the smoky, broke-down shack he called home.

We teased him mercilessly. We listened to his stories like we were interested and, when he finished, called him a liar and laughed at his breathless claims of truth. We plugged our noses when he stood by us in line and slipped bars of soap into his locker. We laughed at his clothes, called him "Scarecrow" and "Patches." Michael also had a learning disability, and we'd mock his stumbling attempts at reading or ask him, pretending seriousness and concern, "How does it feel to be, you know, retarded?" When the Bernards first moved into town, one of the Stensvad girls had been kind to Michael, and he immediately developed a crush on her. We all saw it plain as day—crayoning hearts in his math book, slipping her his chocolate milk at lunch—so some of the boys cornered that girl one recess and ended whatever friendship they had with just a few filthy words. I remember watching Michael follow her around and around the swings days later. She wouldn't so much as look at him.

I was as guilty as the rest. I laughed and joked, pointed and whispered, made fun of everything and anything, avoided sitting by Michael at lunch or throwing him the ball in PE. I was so happy to be one of the boys because I knew that with my home-cut hair, baggy sweaters, and hand-me-down bell-bottoms, I might be next in line. My grandfather was an old man and my father was dead; they couldn't help me any longer. And besides, that thread of acceptance had been gossamer to begin with. My family hadn't homesteaded on the Big Dry or run cattle with one of the ranch outfits in the early days. No, we had moved in after the valley was already settled, my mother was educated, and I wore Payless sneakers. I didn't get invited over for birthday parties or Saturday games of basketball at Tony's or Chip's. I didn't have a father to take me fishing or teach me to ride or show me how to hold the branding iron tight against the skin as the hot metal bit down to flesh. And though I didn't get teased all the time, it happened. How I hated every hot-faced minute of it—someone would yell at me for dropping a pass in football or missing the pitch in kickball, and another boy would sneer and tell me to go read a book. Then, they'd laugh. So like all children who wander along

THE MOUNTAIN AND THE FATHERS

the edges, I looked for, and finally found, by way of cruelty, my way into the middle.

Yet at night, the wind in the chokecherries back of the house, the coyotes calling in the hills, I was tortured by my part in all the teasing and pointing. It would be easy to say I was just a good Catholic boy and bred for guilt, but it was more than that. My father died when I was nine, just a year before Michael and his family moved into town, and with his death I began to live inside myself. While Tony and Chip and most of the other progeny of the Melstone nobility shone like sage gone bright and silver in the sun, their ease in their bodies evident early, their rages red-faced and spitting, their forgiveness quick and whole, I cried when my mother cried, and she cried often. I sat and drank tea with her and talked about the world. I rested in the shade of cottonwoods and read for hours. When angry, I smoldered with indignation for days and pretended showdowns that would never happen outside the red worlds of my imagination. I daydreamed, thought about my father, my mother, this place. I tried so hard to figure it all out: *Why did I always have to be the boy wearing six-dollar sneakers? Was it my mother's fault? My father's? Does a fearful boy turn into a fearful man? Was I weak, destined to lose my father's hard-earned farm and move away? Would I, like him, die young? Would I fail? Or, like the Bernard boys, had I already?*

HE BECAME Carlo in high school. Tony gave him the name. Only Tony could have done it. By fact of birth—heir to an oil fortune on his mother's side and a beautiful jump shot on his father's side—he had unlimited social currency. I don't know what motivated him to do it. Tony was handsome and fun and quick to share his smile with anyone, and it could have been kindness. But he was also unaware of the vicious power he held over other children, and it could have been mere boredom. Whatever the reason, the name stuck. Soon every-one—teachers, coaches, even his mother—called him Carlo. And with this sudden baptism came the blessings of the rest of us. We started sitting by Carlo at lunch, talking to him in the hallways, giving him the ball when he posted up on the block.

It wasn't quite friendship: Carlo became our mascot. We were no longer as mean, but we laughed at him nonetheless. And if Tony said so, Carlo would do just about anything: eat a cricket, moon a car full of girls, pound the rest of that vodka and jump in the freezing river. He knew he had to oblige to stay in our good graces, and he got very good at these things, even started to invent new challenges for himself to further impress us. He'd steal cartons of cigarettes at the Snakepit, clamber up onto the hood of someone's car and piss on their wind-shield, make ridiculously dirty passes at girls. Once, at a bonfire party down on the river, in the middle of a crescendo of beery laughs and country music, Carlo stripped naked except for his shoes and walked into the blaze. I immediately heard a pop and hiss, then caught the stink of melting rubber. As flames leaped around his thighs, I watched him throw back his dark bald head and laugh.

Since we were young, we had all played basketball together. It was a kind of religion: the gymnasium our cathedral, a three-point shot our purest prayer. All of us knew the high plains of eastern Mon-tana offered little else in the way of redemption, knew that to win the Montana State Class C Basketball Championship was to be a kind of low-flying god—like Ronnie Treible or Elvis Oldbull or the Reedpoint team in '94. We heard the stories down at the bar, we read the write-ups in the Billings paper, and Tony, Chip, and Jeff were good enough that we were ranked in the top ten teams in the state all through high school. Yet my senior year, when expectations for us had been highest, we didn't even make the state tournament: We were good, but not good enough.

So, our ascension incomplete and bound to be fleeting, we made up for it however we could: We postured and posed; we strutted down the hallways and winked at freshman girls, told off teachers who gave us As anyway. I discovered that the old men down at the Sportsman and the Mexican loggers who lived in a broken circle of trailers west of town were happy to buy me booze most nights. I'd load up a case of beer and some of the boys in my rickety Toyota Tercel and blast through the windy night up to the oil wells or west on Highway 12 to some other no-account town, where we'd drink and swear and break windows. And though I brought the booze, and Tony could just grin and three girls would slide giggling into the backseat, we always took Carlo along for the ride—because he'd do anything we said and because it always seemed like he was having such a good goddamn time doing it.

One afternoon, on the way to Harlowton again, we stopped at Carlo's house to get a pack of his dad's cigarettes. I drove the Tercel carefully over the ruts in the alley and parked near the chain-link fence. Three snarling dogs came alive, throwing themselves at the latched gate. Jeff, my brother, and I stayed in the car as Carlo jumped out and cursed the dogs, jerked them hard by their rope collars. The dirt yard was littered with engine parts, hunks of wood, dog shit. A deer carcass hung from a cottonwood by the shed. Still holding the dogs, Carlo said his parents weren't home and to come in, there was beer in the fridge. We all filed out, and I was suddenly aware of the fact that none of us had ever been in Carlo's house before. I'd almost forgotten he had a house. He stayed with us or with Tony three or four nights a week. Mrs. Bernard might call, say, on the third night or so, wondering where Carlo was. Or she might not call at all. We seldom saw his parents at our basketball games. His older brother Doug had quit school the year before to go cowboy for an outfit near Rosebud, Henry had been shipped off to a juvenile detention

center in Miles City, and Luke was just another dirty-faced kid staring at us as we ran through our warm-ups during pep rallies. The
stories Carlo now told were almost exclusively about his most recent
drunken silliness. It was like his family and those old stories had just
disappeared.

I have no idea why Carlo invited us in that day, or why we went,
why we stood there, sipping Coors, our eyes adjusting to the unnatu-
ral dark of the front room, or why Carlo didn't hurry us out before we
noticed the overflowing trashcan, the dust-covered TV in the sink, a
wild pattern of colorful stains across the linoleum.

And all the lamps. Two dozen at least. One in the shape of a naked
woman. Another made of driftwood. Some of them missing shades,
others with shades ribboned by scissors or razors, knives, something.
The room was filled with lamps. All of them were dark.

IT WAS after that glimpse inside his house that I became closer to
Carlo. I don't know if it was pity or compassion or kinship, but I
consciously tried to treat him like a real friend. Often, my brother
and I would pick him up in the Tercel, and the three of us would just
drive around and talk. We'd head north on Mosby Road, the smell of
sage and wild onion and blown dust heavy in the air. I'd go on about
whatever I felt like, knowing I wouldn't be made fun of for talking
about novels and liberal politics. My brother would listen and switch
the tapes: Pearl Jam, Tom Petty, Bob Dylan. And Carlo again told
those stories that seemed so fantastic, those stories he'd quit telling
years ago. Now, we never questioned them. They were too lovely,
so long and involved, spanning wars and generations, moving across
years and states into speculation and mystery. I remember only a few
scenes clearly: the loud click of his father's jammed rifle; the weathered face of a man who rode the southwest as an outlaw until he was

well past a hundred years old; the way the trees, bigger than any pine around here, lean in on each other in damp Michigan. Mostly those drives were just a feeling, a rising, a leaving of the known world, if only for a moment.

And as the day went water dark, I'd turn the car around, peg it out at eighty across the flats. We'd stop at the Lazy JC and my brother would run in and buy a round of Gatorades and beef jerky. Then we'd head home, where my mom would put down her book, make a pot of tea, and sit and talk with us. She'd ask Carlo questions and listen carefully to his answers, and his face would light up from the inside.

Though I wouldn't have been able to articulate it then, we had formed an unspoken pact. We knew—especially Carlo and me, as my brother started on the basketball team and dealt with the world around us a bit more easily—we were suspect in the eyes of the other boys at school. On all those late afternoons driving back roads, drinking tea with my mother, we silently vowed not to use our confidences to gain an upper hand with Tony or Chip or anyone else. I had seen the inside of his house, and he had seen the inside of my mind. We protected each other. I stood up beside him and never questioned his stories, treated him as a real friend, not a mascot from across the tracks chosen to moonlight with the cool kids. He stood up beside me and pretended I was just like one of the other guys, not some sissy who looked at the stars and used words like *beautiful*. We never told anyone about the things we admitted to one another: the shame of an ill mother, a dead father, and a place we suspected we either didn't belong or weren't strong enough for.

In his senior year of high school, after a particularly brutal fistfight with his older brother, Carlo more or less moved into our basement and ate meals with us like my mother's third son. I was in my first year of college by then, and though Carlo went home or stayed with someone else now and again, it always seemed like he was at our house when I called home. When he graduated from high school—the first in his family to ever do so—and got accepted into a vo-tech program in Billings, I wrote him a long letter of congratulations, and my brother sold him the Tercel for a dollar so he had a way to get out of town. My mother was so proud of him.

THE SUMMER after my first year at college, I again worked out in the Bull Mountains, on that same cattle, wheat, and dryland hay ranch. I stayed there during the week, in an old homesteader's shack, and took my meals at the main house. The days were long and lonely, but I had done work like this since I was ten, since the summer after my father died—when my mother handed me a shovel and showed me how to kick-start the dirt bike we used for riding ditch banks. With her help, I irrigated our whole place for almost three years, until we leased it out. Then I started working wage jobs. I janitored and mucked out sheds and fixed endless miles of fence, I did twelve-hour days for twenty dollars, I worked whole summers to put just a few hundred in the bank—and I could take it because I knew I wouldn't be doing it forever. In the years after my father died, as I turned slowly in on myself, as I drove those county roads with my brother and Carlo, I decided I was getting out. My mother and my grandfather had long told me I could do it, had long told me that was what I ought to do, and by high school I no longer cared if leasing our land or leaving town meant failure—I no longer cared for the stories of this place. I wouldn't sit for thirty years on a cracked stool at the Sportsman, cursing the weather and reliving the half-court shot that won the game against Ryegate. No, I would leave and go on to what I imagined were bigger and better things.

But that summer, out in the Bulls, I was alone most of the time, walking fence or driving old logging roads, looking for knapweed and toadflax to spray. I felt scattered, nervous—like I'd drunk two shots of cheap whiskey on an empty stomach. This was the third year in a row I'd worked this ranch; I'd wanted to land an internship, to live in a city—but I didn't get any of the positions I applied for, and coming home felt like a defeat.

Out in those scablands there was too much room and time to think. I couldn't help but face the fact that it didn't seem like I belonged at college any more than I did at home. I had struggled in many of my classes my first two semesters. Everyone else had taken AP calculus and physics; I didn't even know what AP meant. And though I had somehow been accepted into the college's honors program, the other students treated me like a circus sideshow, a real-life mountain man from the wilds of Montana. They weren't necessarily mean, but they laughed without restraint at my stories of shotguns and Angus bulls, the Big Dry and high school basketball. They didn't quite believe me, and they sure as hell didn't take me seriously. Worse, when I tried my hand at intellectual conversation, the confident and questioning kind of dialogue that I had long attempted to carry on in my own head, or in the Tercel with my brother and Carlo—they didn't say anything. They smiled and nodded and went on with their conversation. I could tell they were humoring me, I could tell I'd become a kind of mascot.

Of course, I didn't tell any of my friends from Melstone this. I hid it, told them how much fun the college parties were instead. And one weekend in July, the night as dry and hot as the day, I threw a party out at the shack. I got angry drunk that night and swore at a girl I had dated in high school. I tried to fight with Chip, with my brother. Then broke a tequila bottle on the wall and swung the ragged neck of it at whatever was in my way. Later, running senselessly through the dark, I wrapped myself around a barbed-wire fence.

I don't remember any of it. Carlo told me about it the next day. He told me how he and my brother tackled me and pinned me to the wall, how later they convinced me to put the bottle down, and how, when they found me passed out and tangled in the wire, Carlo bent down and picked me up in his big arms and carried me into the shack. He then laid me in a bed and gently pulled my bloody scrap of shirt off me. He held clean towels to my wounds. In the morning, as I sat white-faced and sick at what I'd done, my brother made coffee and Carlo cleaned up the shack. They lit a fire in the trash barrel and burnt the sheets I'd bloodied in the night. Then Carlo helped me to the Tercel and drove us all back to my mother's house.

Right now, if I were to lift my shirt, I could still see those long, white scars. One, two, three across my belly.

WHEN MY brother and I came home from college at Christmas the next year, Carlo was in jail. He'd quit the vo-tech school in Billings and moved back into his parents' place and got into a fight with his brother, Henry. Neighbors heard the threats and screams and called the police. When the cops showed up, Carlo was beating his brother with a two-by-four. Mrs. Bernard swore it was all Carlo's fault. She told them to take him away, said she didn't want him in the house, said she'd testify. After my brother and I heard the story, we scraped together 250 dollars and bailed Carlo out. He came back home with us and never called his family.

So, like we had always done, we drove around and talked, had tea with my mom, sat in the basement and drank whiskey. But I could tell things were different between us. My brother had made friends easily in his first semester at college, and in my second year I too had slowly found a kind of footing. I'd buried myself in books and caught up with my classmates, even done very well here and there. I grew my hair long, traded in jeans for baggy khakis, and started listening to the right kind of music. Though I still didn't feel like I really fit in, I tried to imagine I did. At home, my brother and I talked about college girls, liberation theology, and contemporary fiction, and when we asked Carlo about his program, tried to assure him that he could just go back and start over in January, he shrugged and mumbled and grinned. He seemed happy most of the time, though he didn't tell us any of his stories. Instead, he matched our talk with tales of the high-paying job he was starting in Billings, the many girlfriends he had there.

Though Chip had won an academic scholarship to attend college, he never went. Instead, he bought a trailer, moved it into the pines south of the Musselshell River, and started pouring cement with his father. Over that winter break, Chip threw a lot of parties. And Carlo wanted to go to them all. I went with him, at first, but Chip's parties weren't my parties anymore—everyone listening to Kid Rock and Metallica, arguing about who owed what money for beer and who had how many points in some long-ago basketball game, escorting high school girls to the back bedroom. After finishing off a fifth of vodka one night, Carlo passed out hard. I couldn't lift him to take him to the car. Chip told me to leave him on the couch. He said Carlo had been drinking heavily, doing this a lot lately, and he laughed about how Carlo couldn't keep a job and kept getting turned down by the girls in Billings. "Same old Carlo," he said, and laughed again.

Carlo called the next day to tell us to come over that night, and to bring some beer. We didn't. And Carlo didn't come back to our house that winter. By the time my brother and I left for college, we hadn't seen or heard from him in over a week.

THAT NEXT summer I landed a job in Seattle. I stayed with a college friend whose parents lived in a house on Lake Washington. I worked downtown, wore a shirt and tie, made money. Every day after work my friend and I took his boat out wakeboarding or waterskiing or just cruising around the lakes. Once, we went all the way to Whidbey Island, where his parents had another house. We threw a party there, had a bonfire on the beach, danced to melodic, easy music I had never before heard. Late in the night, the red shadow of burning driftwood playing across her face, a blond-haired girl whose name I've forgotten took my hand in hers and asked me to tell her about Montana. So I did. We lay down next to each other, so close I could taste the smoke and vodka on her breath, and I told her all kinds of stories.

I had no idea life could be like this. At first I was wholly enchanted by the shining skyscrapers downtown, the cool slap of lake water. But the next time I saw that girl at a party, she just waved and walked right by me. She acted like nothing had happened. Or worse, I thought, like what had happened, what we'd said to one another, didn't mean anything. I was staggered, embarrassed. I drank too much. I tried to convince my friend to leave, but he just got annoyed with me. After that, I started working extra hours, eating dinner at some sandwich shop in the city, taking the late bus home. I was reading Joyce for the first time and spent hours sitting on the dock, working my way through a single paragraph. As the sun set over the city's hills, the lake going gold and dark rose, my friend would roar up in his ski boat, see me reading, and shake his head.

Then, in late July, my mother called. She told me Tony had been arrested on another DUI charge and would lose his basketball scholarship for the next year. She paused, and I could tell she was trying not to cry. She told me Carlo's youngest brother, Luke, had lain down in the back bedroom of that house of lamps, nestled the barrel of a shotgun beneath his chin, and, with his toe, pulled the trigger. She told me to say a prayer for Luke, say a prayer for Carlo, and she hung up.

OUT ON the Big Dry, that country that tries to kill you day after day with wind, drought, freeze, and fallow fields—suicide is even worse than government assistance. We know it as Judas's last act, the seal on his damnation, and though there are often some dozen suicides in the forking branches of most rural families, it is still considered a thing near kin to treason, something we do not speak of, a profound and total failure. Suicide bears testament to how god-awful hard it is to live out here. Suicide tells us a bone-deep truth we'd rather not hear: It says we might not be blessed after all. It says our lives—lives so similar to the one that was like an oil-soaked rag thrown away—just might be chance and folly.

When I came back at the end of August, the Bernards had already moved out of town. Carlo came to see us, though. I expected the two of us to drive off in the old Tercel and talk, like we had years ago, but he wanted to see my mother. Over tea at the kitchen table, I sat down with them. At first my mother just asked quiet questions: about Doug and Henry, about the move, about the Tercel. Carlo stared at the table and answered slowly, mechanically. There were spaces of silence. The ache of chair legs on linoleum. A warm wind at the windows, the streaming grass in the fields. But then, as if he had finally decided, Carlo looked up and said that only he and his mother and Luke were home, that he had thought his brother was just mad again and shooting the walls. But when he walked back through the hall to tell him to knock it off, he saw blood and his young brother's still body and the barrel of the gun wet with blood. He said he grabbed his mother as she was coming back to see what had happened and carried her out the door, then scrambled back inside and locked her out. She screamed and cried and demanded to know what happened, what he'd done, what Carlo had done to Luke.

He was crying now, his big shoulders hitching and trembling, and the story halted and skipped in time. Soon he was helping his parents move into a house near the Snowy Mountains, and his mother was still in rough shape, but they were all going to church and doing a little better, and he was thinking of working on a ranch out there, and finally he told us Luke hadn't written a note, but he had ordered, through some kind of delivery service on the internet, a series of cards and flowers to be sent to his mom. Mrs. Bernard got the first note and bouquet for her birthday, just a few short weeks after the funeral.

My mother didn't say a word through Carlo's story. After, while Carlo stared at the dark tea cold in his cup, his face wet with snot and tears, she took his hand and my hand, and she said a blessing for the repose of Luke's soul. And she went on. She prayed for a long time, she prayed for many things. The plains wind worried the windows.

FIFTEEN YEARS ago I left the Big Dry. I haven't branded cattle or walked even a mile of fence in years. Last spring my mom got a fair offer and sold the farm. By most counts, I have failed the place of my birth. In my first years away, passing this very judgment on myself, I tried hard to hate the place of my boyhood. I blamed it for so many things—disaffections, drunken violence, deaths. I thought it did terrible damage to me, to Carlo, even to Tony, Chip, and Jeff, to anyone who tried to rise above the notions and destructions of that land of dust.

Yet all things change and do not change: The river ran full and brown and foaming this last spring. My mother told me over the phone, in a voice I know well, that she'd never seen such wind. The oil wells have dried up. Some out-of-state company wants to rip into the Bull Mountains for coal again. Many old families have sold out and moved on. Rich Californians looking for good elk hunting have moved in. The Sportsman Bar closed down. A couple of high school kids opened a mobile espresso stand.

When I come to visit, people stop and ask if I remember a certain long-ago basketball game, catch me up on the local gossip. They ask about me, about my studies and where they have taken me. They are kind and concerned. And so I tell them the truth: I'm in Iowa now, in a college town that gives way to a brimming river and long fields of corn. I am a teacher and the work suits me. I've married a wonderful woman. We have two children, a little boy and a baby girl. When we visit Montana, we hike the buttes and ridges south of the river. We listen for the clear cries of meadowlark, kneel down and run our hands through the pine duff. On summer afternoons, we sit on my mother's porch and watch storms roll west, see the sky go white with lightning, shake with thunder. At midnight, we stand on the rutted stretch of gravel that leads to the house and crane our necks back to look at the great wash of stars that is more beautiful and strange than I ever remember. Last spring, while we trimmed weeds and arranged flowers, my son played in the dirt atop the graves of his grandfather and his great-grandfather.

The world is not as I thought it was. I do not think I will ever know it.

SINCE THAT day in my mother's kitchen, I've only seen Carlo two or three times. The last was some years ago now, during my final year of college. My brother and I had brought some friends home over the Christmas holiday. On New Year's Eve, we all drove out to the Jersey Lily. It's on the way to nowhere, out in the heart of the Big Dry, but, of course, Carlo just happened to show up. He was grinning, as always, and gave us big hugs and sat down and drank and acted as happy as ever. With all the laughter and chatter, I only got a chance to talk with him a little. He bragged about how much money he was making as a contractor, how much fun he was having at the bars up in Billings. I asked about his family, about his mother. It was a little over two years since Luke had killed himself, and he told me, "Fine. They're just fine."

I remember, through the clatter of whiskey bottles and Waylon Jennings's jukebox growl, wondering, and hating myself for wondering, if anything he told me was true.

MY WIFE has gone to bed, and I have set down my book. The Iowa dark is at my window. I hear, now and then, through the static of the monitor, the breathing of my children. I rise and pace our front room, pour a glass of whiskey. In childhood, when I could not sleep, when the world troubled me and set my mind to racing, my mother would tell me to say a prayer, to pray for those I love until sleep took me—for when it did the angels would finish my prayers. "The angels," she would say, "cannot refuse a sleeping child." But I am no longer a child, and I do not believe all I believed as a boy.

All those years ago, on the phone, Carlo told me he wanted me to know how sad and ashamed he was when he thought about all the awful things he used to do, and he was, I am sure, telling me the truth. I should have told him the truth, should have reminded him of the time he carried me in my shame. I have no way, save cowardice, to account for this. For I am completely grateful. Many hands have held me. And I am here, and who I am, because of them. How then do we reach out to those who have saved us, those who have delivered us from ourselves and unto ourselves?

My mother prays. I try to tell our story.

And I end it now, because I can, in Montana, where the wind snaps the prairie grass and with the dust the sharp smell of wild onion rises. Here, Carlo, I do what I could not on the phone: I lift my arms to you in greeting. I see you, and I see, too, that sadness is fine. This journey has been a dark one. Yet I pray someday each lamp may finally click on, and the world stream with seventy-watt glory, stream and fill with a kind of gentle fire.

My Mother's Story,
Part Two

WHAT I AM trying for here is the sound of her voice.

Earlier this evening, I called my mother and asked her about my father. I don't know why. Maybe because I seldom ask, maybe because all that was some time ago and it seems now safe to speak of it. Anyway, I asked, and though I do not know exactly what I expected, I did not hear it.

I heard my father's name said in sudden wonder. I heard laughter, a lover's grace. Her voice softened and slowed, began to move with some glad rhythm, like a song on the radio you haven't heard in years but know you've loved before—that half-remembered first note, the wild refrain.

It was her voice. It was her voice that set me down to writing. This is my mother's story. Or, more accurately, this is my telling of my mother's story, the story of how she met my father, of how the two of them came to be my parents.

This is about the way even those you feel you know, you don't.

This is about the broken world, those the world breaks.

This is about the way a story stoops and gathers up the pieces.

This is about the sound of a woman's voice. *It was May*, she said, *of 1970. He wore a snap shirt, collar on his shoulders. And there were flowers, and mountains, and—hold on. I'm getting all mixed up. Let me start again.*

I sure liked the way he talked, but I didn't even know him. I wasn't sure I could believe a thing he said! My mother paused for the first time here, took a moment to catch her breath. I heard her shift the phone a bit and suddenly remembered who she was, that she was talking about herself. I had forgotten for a moment that this was not just another story—but her story.

Yet that pause, that charged space of silence, I'll make that mine. For even now—hours later, in my office, splash of streetlight at my window—I can close my eyes and see her standing on the kitchen's cracked linoleum, her weight shifted over to her one good hip, the plains wind at the duct-taped window, see her begin again her story.

SHE WAS still on the dance floor, still talking about Johnny Cash with this young and handsome man she barely knew—but she couldn't help herself. This happy remembering was too much. She began to jumble time, told me they didn't talk about marriage that summer, or the next fall, but she thought about it a lot.

I was only half listening. With that embrace at Bar 17, that slow dance, already my part in this story was beginning.

I could see those tired faces I memorized on autumn nights, moonlight pooling through the windows. He would be in the easy chair in the front room, laid back, his bony feet and ankles sticking out awkwardly from beneath a wool blanket. There was the rasping sound of her calloused hand over his stubbled jaw, then along the back of his bald and flaking head. It was always so hot, right up until winter, which was when he went to the hospital for good.

Each of his unintelligible cries pulled me from some cool dream of river water back into my twisted, sweat-damp sheets. Only her touch and the sibilance of her shushes calmed him, calmed me.

How able she was, how in control.

Yet when they danced, he took the lead.

On the phone tonight the words spilled so quickly from her, as if of their own volition, as if story has some power over lips and minds and limbs: *Dancing*, she was saying, *every night that week. He came in every night that week and took me dancing.*

TWO-DOLLAR CHAMPAGNE, she said. *We drank it out of soda bottles and then drove all through the night.* She was caught up yet in memory, a bride on her happy, hopeful way to the rainy Pacific Northwest, but I was watching her step through the dry stalks of a drought-killed field, my little brother crying on her hip. I was wondering how the world goes so wrong, how this mountain of joy ends up in acres of sun-blown dust.

Theodicy, believers call it: the wondering and explaining, the wrestling with what one must understand as God's justice, with the fact that a good and knowing God has chosen for some of us this, and for some of us that, has said, *I give you life. I give you life. And you, I give you pain.*

Can we trust any God fickle and vicious as this? And what are we to do then with our fathers and our mothers, our first and mightiest gods?

HERE, MY mother's voice broke for the first time. He had brought her back to Montana, to the Big Dry, and she was running out of happy memories. She was so suddenly close to the end of all this—there in place, soon to be in time.

She used to lecture my brother and me, telling us, after one of our frequent fights—our eyes red and wet, our jeans dirty and torn—that we had to save our strength, that together we had to fight this hard world. She told us no one would give us anything, that we had to work for everything, had to get good grades at school and save our summer wages so someday we could go to college and choose what lives we wanted for ourselves. We couldn't mess around, she told us, with nonsense like fistfights or rodeo riding or the smooth glass of whiskey bottles, as all of that would only hold a body here, would only chain us to this place.

And, for the most part, we believed her. I read all the time. I'd lie down for hours under the cottonwoods with the pages of a book my sky; I'd find a corner of the house and disappear into Narnia or war-torn Spain for days. I studied hard and wrote essays and even won trips to conferences and competitions. By eighteen I had traveled, in my patched jeans and dusty tennis shoes, from one coast to the other. My brother, a year behind me, did just as well in school and started on the basketball team, too. And by that time, my older sister was already off at college.

Yet it was anything but easy. Truly, my quickest, first memories of growing up out on the Big Dry are of walking each day to the dry river, tromping through our sun-bitten fields, the dust rising even with my small boy's scuffs and steps. Or my mother, down on a knee, her hands in that very dust. Though she kept the worst of it from us, we couldn't help but notice her arguing over this bill or that bill, the way she made do with dull kitchen knives and never a new dress and to this day the same stained, broken-backed furniture. Until I was maybe thirteen or so, I could count the number of times I'd eaten out on my two hands. In the evenings, I'd read by whatever light was left, even in the starry dark, just to keep that electric bill low, to save money, to feel like I was helping. And always I remember wondering, hashing it out with my sister and my brother: Why were we so poor? What had we done? Why couldn't we buy new Levi's or eat at the café in town?

The summer after my father died was the driest in years, the grasshoppers whirring through the grass, smoke from the great fires in Yellowstone in all our eyes. Two reporters from *The Boston Globe* knocked on our door and told us a neighbor sent them over. They were after stories of the drought. They were sorry, they said, to hear about my father. My mother let them in, served iced tea at the kitchen table. From the hallway that was our room, my brother and I spied and wondered. The lady reporter sat on the edge of her chair; she was angular and sophisticated, her skin the color of creamed coffee. The man was slender in the chest and looked as if he'd never in his life been tired. Boston? They may as well have been from the moon.

My mother was telling them our story. Soon, she was crying, and the reporter was crying, and the photographer stood there with his camera forgotten in his hands. Later, he took a picture of us in the field: my mother, still slender, her hair lifting a bit in the plains wind, and the dry, cracked soil of what was supposed to be a pasture of alfalfa beneath her feet. In the far corner, in my mother's long shadow, I sat sifting dust.

Even though the neighbors sent those reporters to our house, it wasn't just us. That was our summer of grief, but others had it just as bad. The Big Dry was a place of tremendous ruin. I saw it all around. Bryan, driving fast and wild one night after a rodeo, got T-boned by a trucker making time down Highway 12; they held his funeral in the school gymnasium, and I remember that Doug Bernard, the toughest kid in school, ran out crying. My friend Chip robbed a liquor store two towns over and did time. I see him now and again when I am in Montana; he's kind and quiet. Like Randy, who went to high school with my older sister and was going to play basketball for the community college but failed out after his first semester—he pulled a trailer up into the hills and settled in to buying beer for high school kids. One of my brother's old girlfriends worked for years at a strip club. One of mine, whose long, strawberry hair fell nearly to her belt, took up with some cowboy from Oklahoma, and when she tried to leave him, he drove her out onto the prairie and shot her dead.

This is the Big Dry—the railroads gone, the oil gone, the rain never falling—yet like most any place of deep poverty and latent violence, the worst of it is that slow erosion of imagination, of any hope for something better. So, if you are, say, a boy who lives inside your head, or a girl who dreams of peace and other silly possibilities—you better knock it off, you better step into this: the only world you'll ever know.

But she said no. She had us, my brother and me, by the dirty collars of our shirts, and she knelt down. She said this isn't the way it's going to be. She said there's something better. She said to keep dreaming. So we did. And like our older sister, we made it out—we left for college and left her there. Left her there alone. It's the way I thought it had to be. But in her story, her voice, I hear what possibilities she once had. I hear, like us, she left.

Why come back? If this were all there was, that would be one thing—but she came back, of her own volition. She chose it all again. Or, she chose him, he chose the land, and then, I guess, some god said, *Suffer*.

What if she'd said no that time before? What if she'd said anything? Though she pushed us hard as hell to get out, she followed him back in. She followed him.

THE YEARS go by with nothing. Still, they try for a son, she tells me, because they have faith, and they have faith—the stubborn faith that says wet years on a land everyone calls the Big Dry will stay, that says the world is good and so is God and they are young and strong and blessed. She tells me now they want a son, and I want her to stop this story: No, I want this story for myself.

I'll tell it the way I want to tell it, the way it should have been: I'll tell them to get out of there, to go back to Seattle, Durango, anywhere. Tell her to take him to a VA hospital because there is a poison in his veins. Those chemicals they washed across the land, when he was in the army and on their very fields, are in him now—they're attacking his cells right now, and those idiot country doctors in Roundup are wrong: It's not ulcers. It's cancer. I know all this, know there are years of hardscrabble, dry-river poverty to come, know what they should have done—but he's the one.

Even if this story's mine, it's not. Tonight, on the phone, my mother told me the story of my birth, which always becomes his story—the birth of his son: He is dead, and I am his son.

THE LAST words, too, are always his.

He hands me to her, speaks to her, and then he leaves the hospital, and here is where my mother finished her story. Her voice, then, was the voice I am used to, that of a woman near seventy, a widow longer than a wife. She worried over the president, asked about the weather, told me that it finally rained last week and her garden needed it.

But she did not tell me who held whom in the night, or how tired he was, or how, when he could no longer dance, his bones too fragile, Dom Barsilucci, in his charitable stupidity, kept asking her to dance, dancing with her, holding her, while on the jukebox Waylon sang "Amanda" and Cash sang "Without Love," and he was angry and tired and angry—and there was nothing he could do about it. She did not tell me that his skin flaked off in sheets, that his thick chest and shoulders hollowed and shrunk, that he wept, like a child, when she had to hitch his pants up with bailing twine. How he weighed even less than her when he died.

She did not tell me these things. I've heard them before, from my older sister, who saw it all and was old enough to remember; from my Uncle Lawrence and Jack Peters; from the old men at the Sportsman Bar who clap me on the shoulder and say again and again that they are sorry, say what a damn shame.

But this night I wanted something more, something anecdote and drunken commiseration cannot give. I wanted to know why. I wanted to know if it was worth it. For her. For us. If the suffering we shared and shouldered was too much.

So I asked: I asked my mother if she thought they made the right decisions, if maybe they should have stayed in Durango with the steady paycheck and good health care and hospitals, if the hand-to-mouth and day-to-day way of life we endured in the years after my father's death could have been otherwise, if maybe her hard and reckless push to get us out of that place and into college could have been easier, if she herself wouldn't rather grow old somewhere else, if maybe she would like to look through a window not cracked and patched with duct tape, if maybe beyond the window she would like to see a world mostly whole as well—not those corrals her young husband built falling every day farther down. If she doesn't wish—for even a moment—to grow old with someone else.

No, she said. *No. Haven't you been listening?*

She told me that one day in that last October, when he was sick and getting sicker—*and you must remember this?*—all the farmers down the valley loaded their trucks with good lumber and nails and drove out to our place and framed out a massive machine shed, and their

206

wives fixed fried chicken and green bean salad for lunch, and everyone worked all day and finished that barn right up to the tin roof—
and they left us then that evening with bowls of food and prayers, and
that barn still stands today.

She said, *Anyway, I loved him. I love him.*

She was quiet a moment. She said goodbye and hung up.

ON COOL mornings, my mother drives out onto the plains and steps
into the wind of the Big Dry. She walks slowly, a slight hitch in her step
from a bad hip. Like a man, she wears a ball cap to keep the sun out of
her eyes. She studies the ground, gets down on a knee now and then
and runs her hands through the dirt. She is looking for fossils, Precam-
brian fish and nautilus and snail, the stone evidence of ancient oceans.
With her thumb she wipes dust from the stones. She drives home and
makes a cup of tea and prays and rests in the heat of the afternoon on
the couch. She reads and tends her garden. She retired not long ago
from thirty years of teaching school, and this last spring the senior class
asked her to give a speech at their graduation. She just finished a college course on magazine writing at the branch university in Billings,
which she enjoyed, though she is not sure she'll take another because
of the drive. Every other summer she flies to Minneapolis to visit an
old friend from college. She has sold the farm, though she still stays in
the old house, had it written into the contract that she could live there
as long as she wanted. She is letting go of her grief, which I understand
now is her love, in steps. She takes care of her mother, who still lives
down the road, though near-blind and ninety-three. She is always, it
seems, taking care of someone. And each Sunday she calls in turn her
three children—now grown and gone so far away.

Hours ago, I put down the phone. I cannot see the stars, the sky
laved by streetlights. I think, *It doesn't matter.*

I think, *No, it all matters. The life I lead is the one she wanted for me. The only gods must be mothers in love with fathers.*

I think, *Yes, what we must call gods are good days, and the stories of those fleeting, too-few days.*

Oh God, I think, *for those good days must we bite every sorrow, and then some more?*

He is dead, I think, *but I am alive. I must finish our story.*

OUR FATHERS

THEY FAIL US, our fathers.

You, Father, failed by leaving. And you, Father, by being more than I could ever be. You by being less. You in your undivided silence. You in your unbridled love. You in your rigor, your sadness and strength, your wisdom, word, and sloth. You in your grief.

You, all of you, with your windblown faces and slumped shoulders, hands like hunks of pine—you are this way in the world and you are that way in the world and which way should I be? Which way? You won't say. You storm and suffer, tremble and shine, say goodbye, goodbye.

You die.

I'm damn sick of loving you, damn sick of being you—but fathers, help me. For just now, from across the measureless galaxies of blood and good, good fortune, I have heard the sound of my own son's grain-of-sand heart; that tidal surge and lunge; that whoosh and susurrus, a slight wind whispering that some warm and ripping storm is building, has begun.

Fathers, forgive me.

And you, little clot of cells, little mumble of mother's blood, little swimming screamer, my unborn son, forgive nothing. All this is without your permission. Hold it against me—hold and know, know your fathers. Know whatever wings we wear, we must take them off in the end. Know we have chosen whatever betrayals and loves we live with. Know we love, even when we seem not enough with love. Know we know so very little.

I will tell you this: Long before the world was fashioned, the fathers gathered in the valley of the river that came down from the mountain. Before the many dangers of the mountain, the fathers were naked, they stood dazzled and confused.

Little one, we are here!

The Field

HERE IS THE sun breaking over the far hills and trees. Here is the field, the alfalfa tall and leafy and wet with dew. See the man seated on the still-cool swather, with that green-and-white-mesh ball cap set high on his head of dark curls? See how he leans over the swather's steering bars and watches the shadows break and drift? That is my father. He is thirty-six years old. He is strong and handsome, his body his own. It is late July, haying season, and he is waiting for the sun to dry the dew from the field. He is happy just waiting, happy because in this dry country too much moisture is a fine problem to have, because a meadowlark is calling, because the air this morning is sweet and sharp with clover and sage.

He is happy as well because he knows at lunch his wife will make him a tomato sandwich with lots of pepper and mayonnaise. He will eat it over the sink, letting the good mess of it run down his wrists and sunburnt arms and drip from his elbows. He will wash and play Legos on the floor with his daughter, before sending her to her nap. He will step down into the basement then, where the walls are stone and cool. He will pass the pine shelves stacked with mason jars of pickled beets, chokecherry syrup, beef tongue. Stretched rectangles of light will spill from the high, inset windows. Near the great mouth of the swamp cooler, he will sit on the floor by the hi-fi and his box of records. He will play some Waylon Jennings and some Johnny Cash, finish with Gordon Lightfoot. He will close his eyes and sing along, just under his breath: *They say you've been out wandering. They say you've traveled far. Sit down, young stranger, and tell us who you are . . .*

And his wife, this kind and slender woman, will come quietly down the stairs and sit on the easy chair behind him. They will laugh and smile at some small thing and listen to the music while she works at the knots in his shoulders. And, when the album has spun into silence and their talk has died down and the swamp cooler ticks, motes of dust sifting and sliding through the subterranean light, he will turn to look at her, and slip his arms around her, and pull her to him.

Do you see him? My father in his happiness? I have put him there not for you but for me. I need to see now that it's possible. I need to see how this happiness is lived. All this is for me.

For him? What will I do for him? This is what I will do:

I leave him now, in the field.